PQ

How it matters more than IQ

W0043145

PQ

How it matters more than IQ

Virender Kapoor

BLOOMSBURY
LONDON • NEW DELHI • NEW YORK • SYDNEY

Copyright © 2015 Virender Kapoor

All rights reserved.

No part of this publication may be reproduced or transmitted in any form or by any means, electronic or mechanical, including photocopying, recording, or any information storage or retrieval system, without prior permission in writing from the publishers.

No responsibility for loss caused to any individual or organization acting on or refraining from action as a result of the material in this publication can be accepted by Bloomsbury India or the authors/editor.

Bloomsbury Publishing India Pvt Ltd

Vishrut Building, DDA Complex
Building No. 3, Pocket C-6 & 7, Vasant Kunj
New Delhi 110 070
www.bloomsbury.com

Bloomsbury is a registered trademark of Bloomsbury Publishing Plc

ISBN: 978-93-84052-53-9
10 9 8 7 6 5 4 3 2 1

Typeset by Eleven Arts
Printed and bound by Replika Press Pvt Ltd

The content of this book is the sole expression and opinion of its author, and not of the publisher. The publisher in no manner is liable for any opinion or views expressed by the author. While best efforts have been made in preparing this book, the publisher makes no representations or warranties of any kind and assumes no liabilities of any kind with respect to the accuracy or completeness of the content and specifically disclaims any implied warranties of merchantability or fitness of use for a particular purpose.

The publisher believes that the content of this book does not violate any existing copyright/intellectual property of others in any manner whatsoever. However, in case any source has not been duly attributed, the publisher may be notified in writing for necessary action.

Contents

Media Reviews

Maharashtra Herald: '*PQ How it matters more than IQ*' talks about the most important strength of human beings.'

Times of India: 'This book by Kapoor portrays the true meaning of the often used phrase , 'Fire n the belly'.'

Sunday Pioneer: 'This book effectively demonstrates that enthusiasm and passion rather than college degrees and high IQ are most sought after for peak performance.'

Times of India: India Time's best seller: 'This book will show you how to raise your Passion Quotient for achieving success'.

The Hindu Business Line: 'Offers more than a dozen tips to bring back that fizz into your current job. It can make you walk that extra mile − without effort.'

DNA: 'The author provides innovative strategies to hone the hidden talent and creative instincts.'

Hindustan Times: 'Most ordinary people have become very successful by simply doing what they wanted to do. PQ matters more than IQ.'

DNA Money: 'This book shatters the myth that college degree & high IQ are the major drivers.'

Indian Express: 'Crafted in simple language, the book talks about cultivation and nurturing of passion.'

Outlook business: 'Between its pages, one can encounter many a nugget of wisdom on what constitutes passion.'

Tribune: 'This book helps you to find your perfect cup of tea.'

Education Times: 'The crux of the book lies in that it is not IQ but PQ which will take you to the pinnacle of success.'

Deccan Herald: 'Establishes the fact that with conscious efforts we can identify what we like and what we don't. Virender Kapoor has firmly established the concept of PQ and gives a new meaning to our driving force.'

Hindustan Times: 'If you don't read Virender Kapoor's '*PQ How it matters more than IQ*', you just might find yourself in the gutters. A ready reckoner, it is a guide to your PQ.'

Preface

Hundreds, and may be thousands of books have been written and are still being written on success, winning strategies, leadership, influencing people, and making friends, or interpersonal skills and so on. Most of them talk about laws, and habits, which make people successful.

What motivated me to write this book was the fact that there is very little organised literature available about 'passion', and how to follow your heart to be successful. It is also intriguing that every book on motivation talks about this aspect, without giving any worthwhile inputs on the subject.

This surprised me because that really is the driving energy behind every activity. It is one of the strongest emotions available to human beings. Had there been no passion, the human race wouldn't have come into existence, and wouldn't have proliferated, as it has over the millions of years of our existence.

The second reason for writing this book was that, the time has come when we can afford to experiment. The opportunities available today are far greater than what were available three to four decades ago. In the sixties, population in India was around 33 million, and one had very few options beyond engineering, medicine, chartered accountancy, or a government job. Today, the population is a little over 1,000 million (three times the earlier mark), whereas, opportunities and types of professions/vocations have gone up by 50 times, if not more. Mass communication, ITEs, consultancy, telecom, show business, catering, hotel industry, and airlines, to name a few, have all proliferated to unbelievable scales. Many of us have gone far beyond the *Roti, Kapda, aur Makan* syndrome – so it's time to experiment.

I have met a lot of people – especially in the last 10 years – who have been *happily successful,* by taking on a profession which they actually wanted to be in. This was another convincing reason to write this book. Thus, in net effect, this is liberalisation – we are today liberalised to follow our heart.

Passion in isolation would be like a genie locked up in a bottle. It has to come in contact with our other attributes, like vision, skills, creativity, and determination, to make any worthwhile impact on our lives.

Combined with all our other abilities, it should be able to help us achieve what we want to achieve. I am convinced that it is the single most important ingredient for success. Passion for success means two things – you must be passionate about success, and to be successful, you must be passionate. While working on this, it became clear to me that it is required from KG to PG during the days of our education, and is also important for executives, entrepreneurs, political leaders, industrialists, and even philanthropists. So, the applicability bandwidth is pretty broad.

I have given enough examples of people from different walks of life and professional domains, to demonstrate that the best thing would be to follow your likes and bring that fizz to your life.

It also became clear that with conscious efforts, we can identify what we like, and what we don't, which becomes the first step forward. You need not be madly in love with something to start with, but constant efforts can always bring very positive results. Eventually, you should be able to say for yourself, 'I live to work and not work to live'.

I am sure the readers would greatly benefit by reading this book, and will be able to identify their strong likes and dislikes, and venture into areas which will bring them happiness, bliss, and success!

Virender Kapoor

Introduction

Almost every book and literature on success and motivation talks about 'passion', in some context or the other. It becomes the propelling force for professionals, entrepreneurs, musicians, actors, lawyers, pilots, writers, scientists, fashion designers, and almost every conceivable human profession. On the personal front, to do up your home, making a marriage work, organising fashion shows in college, a picnic with friends, making a rockery in your garden, going for a long drive, getting your body in shape, and even wooing your girlfriend or boyfriend; all require only one element-passion. In schools and colleges, students who are enthusiastic about a subject, spend more time learning that subject without getting tired of it, and hence, score the highest marks in that subject. It is not unusual to hear someone say, 'I love maths', and the other one saying 'I hate French, can't understand a word of it!'. Many science buffs who are in awe of science, love physics, but hate chemistry! All this is to do with your inner inspiration.

It gets linked directly to inner motivation which is a guiding spirit for self-motivated successful people. It is an all important ingredient for leadership as well. Successful leaders are always excited about whatever they are into. Surprisingly, there is very little practical information available to a reader, regarding passion and all its facets. One keeps hearing advices like, 'follow your passion', 'work passionately', and 'identify your passion'. But nobody tells you how to do all that. There is, therefore, a need to look at it as a whole, and in an integrated way—making it practical, useful and application-oriented, rather than its present form with a 'halo' around it.

In seminars, I ask a simple question like, 'What is your passion?' Surprisingly, it baffles many of the participants. Some people come and ask me, whether it is a must to have it. Many of them don't know how to identify it, and there are many who clearly see it, but don't know what to really do about it. How to put into practise what they love is a dilemma with many. Some of them feel that they like something, but they don't know if it is really passion, or something else. What about those who have no passion? Can we generate or kindle it? They ask.

Most importantly, one would like to know, how to get excitement into your work, at home, your workplace, and in your life in general. Even if a book can raise your Passion Quotient (PQ) by 20%, it would change your life. Life will become more meaningful, more enjoyable, and of course, it will catapult your productivity to heights you could never ever imagine reaching – that too without feeling the effort. It would act like a 'virtual energy', which existed, but you were not aware of it.

Passion is a very strong expression. It resides in your heart, and in the pit of your stomach, maybe in the rest of your vibrant body – but certainly not in your head! Also, many a times it doesn't see reason. It is an emotion, and therefore, is part of emotional competence. Human emotions unfortunately cannot be singled out or compartmentalised, as they are interlinked. At best, you can make clusters of closely-related emotions. It finds its direct connectivity with enthusiasm, excitement, drive, arousal, grit, motivation, and even obsession, to name a few.

Jupiter not wanting mans life to be wholly gloomy
and grim has bestowed far more Passion than reason.
Moreover, he confined reason to a cramped corner
of the head and left all the rest of the body to the Passions.

- Desiderius Erasmus

Human emotions cannot be measured accurately. You cannot, therefore, assign a number or a figure to it, as in the case of Intelligence Quotient (IQ). Yet, one finds expressions like 'Arousal Quotient', 'Fashion Quotient', 'Fun Quotient', or say 'Activity Quotient', being used in some context or the other. These are at best notional, indicative, and representative in nature. In this book, I have used the expression 'Passion Quotion' in a similar spirit.

Creativity and stimulation are highly connected areas of human excellence. Creativity may not technically fall under the realm of emotions, but it certainly gets infused, activated, and blossoms with the support of an enthusiastic attitude. You would always find creative people very involved in what they do. In fact, passion generates creativity, and creativity needs passion. With all the connected, clustered emotions and creativity, it could well be called 'Passionology'. It is like a spoon of curd that sets a bowl of milk into curd. One spoon of passion in your life could change the context and content of life. Try it.

About This Book

It is about getting fired up, and bringing some fizz into your life, your workplace, home, and your attitude! There can be a depressive 'lousy attitude', which not only messes up your own happiness and productivity, but also bumps others on their heads. You not only have to make your attitude positive – as everybody talks about it – but you need to 'brighten' up your attitude as well! Yes, you can brighten up your attitude and your life with excitement. This book is about stimulating your mind. As I said earlier, passion and creativity are closely-related areas of human excellence. Creativity without a dash of enthusiasm would lose out on its sheen. In fact, passion can fire up that creative genius which all of us to some degree possess. This book will guide you to get that rust off your skin, and polish your creative prowess. It is a practical guide and a working manual, which would help infuse more life into your life, enabling you to live life to the fullest. This book will help you find your strengths, your likes, and your intrinsic energy, and will take you to the heights that you deserve to attain. This will bring you name, fame, and success. Do you need more?

What Would a Reader Get Out Of This Book

This book will teach you how to raise your Passion Quotient. First, it should answer some basic questions and clear the fog. What is passion? Is it a must to have it? How do I generate it if I don't have some of it yet? Is it hardwired into us from birth, or can it surface at anytime and at any age? Second, it should become a guide and a source to identify your strong likes, and give you ideas to generate passion, and implement it in your organisations and at your homes. How to stimulate a child's mind is an important aspect, and this book will show you how to do it. Third, it should give you an idea as to where you stand today on Passion Quotient, and give you abroad direction to move on.

Most importantly, it would give readers courage to use their strengths productively. In addition, it would show simple ways of bringing excitement into ones work, moving towards more meaningful, individual life, and ultimately raising your Passion Quotient. It would also help those fence-sitters make up their mind. All those who have retired from very active professions must spend their time well. Often you feel you worked all your life doing what somebody else told you to do and you had to do it because you had to do it: financial constraints, family compulsions, lack of direction and guidance at the right time, not enough opportunities at appropriate time in life, few options to choose from during those days, etc. People do look at second careers to do what they wanted to do, but were unable to, because of the reasons cited before. There could be an interesting twist in your life after retirement. This book would give you the conviction, the direction, and that slight nudge, that is required to get into a love affair – an affair with life. This book would show you how to do all this. And last but not the least, how to become more creative and live life to the fullest.

Who Should be Reading This Book

Who would not like to improve upon his IQ? Every one would love to have a higher IQ, whatever be the cost. Similarly, every individual would love to raise their PQ, whatever be the efforts. Unfortunately, IQ comes more like a hardwired DNA bonanza, which you cannot really improve upon, whereas, you can raise your PQ threshold and become more creative, by making some conscious efforts. Let me mention here that people with high IQ who were low on Passion and drive have rarely made it to the top. Albert Einstein, who was very high on IQ had tremendous love for whatever he did. I think, the fire in the belly, another term for zing, contributed more to Einstein's success, than his high IQ! Reading this book would help in delving into deeper convictions, to find your latent or unexplored talents.

This book would be very appealing and useful for the students who, while graduating from school, want to decide which line of education they should choose. It would also be of immense use to those, who after graduation, want to get into a professional PG course. Today, there are enough options and variants available to pursue, and do what you love doing. At a professional level, it would be helpful to people from all verticals who want to raise their PQ, bring zing to their jobs, and become more productive at workplace. School teachers, trainers, and academicians, will get some ideas to infuse some fizz into their disciples. Parents would learn how to foster this virtual energy, and creativity into their children.

Today as our economy is booming, new opportunities are popping up, new professions are emerging, and application of technology and opportunities are limited only by our imagination. In this scenario, everybody would like to improve his or her lot, and passion could play a pivotal part in this transformation. Raise your Passion Quotient and raise a toast – cheers!

How to Read This Book

You got to be serious if you want to add excitement and give meaning to your life. You also got to be serious if you want to be creative and successful. So I urge you to read this book seriously. Take a pencil and underline areas that are directly relevant to you, jot down some notes on the margins, and all the time, while reading, relate yourself with what is being said – be there. And do attempt all the questions that are given at the end of each chapter. If you do all this, you would be able to get the maximum bang for the buck, as they say.

I have made this a very simple reading. All aspects have been backed by short stories, examples of relevant people, anecdotes, and some questions to be answered at the end of each chapter. It is practical and not a theoretical discourse. So read on.

Having read the book, go for the PQ test given at the end of the book. Once you are done with the book, you will be in a better position to understand the questions, and answer them more objectively

PQ—Journey Till Now and the Road Ahead

The pace at which the world is changing, and the speed at which technology is reinventing itself, has been tremendous in the last few years.

Since there was no book on passion per se, it was a lonely journey and full of apprehensions too. There were very few goal posts, landmarks, or even bouys available, to go by. Yet the content came out to my entire satisfaction.

In the last few years, I gained more experience, and could review my work and revisit it from several different angles.

I also wrote four more books in the area of human excellence during these years, which broadened my vision as well. These ranged from work-life balance, leadership, personal victory, and jugaad attitude.

Having headed a prestigious business school for around a decade, I had the privilege of interacting with young and bright students who came from different parts of the country. I moved on in life to start a business school of my own with full support of the industry. As a founder, this gave me the autonomy to lay down my own mission and my operational ground rules, to fulfill my vision. I wanted to practice what I preach, and of course I did. It is worthwhile to look at the performance pyramid of the job-seeking youth in this context. One serious look tells you that only a very few are distinguished students, if you look at the academic performance alone. Therefore, the number of people who can make it to top B-schools is very small. Only a very small fraction of the total number of aspirants gets there.

Two questions that need to be answered are, 'Do only those students, who go to top B-schools, make it big in life? And how do you help those who are not traditionally or academically intelligent?'

My experience tells me that those who are 'academically bright' do have an edge over those who we think are not. How do we push those who are not academically so inclined, up the performance pyramid? As educationists, how do we contribute to the economy of the nation? We are the HRD people; we develop the human resource for the industry, which is a major contributor to the national might.

Therefore, it is our job to see that we take academically average students, and make them perform extraordinarily in their lives. This has been the focus of my experiment and experience for the last few years. I have closely observed the performance of students, especially their behaviours, to map it to their performance; on and off campus. Closely examining the performance of our alumni, whom we mentor while they are on campus, also indicates that academic performance alone is not the winning edge. While EQ plays a very critical role, and is an important parameter in the performance equation of an individual, there is something not yet known, that can literally turn the tables.

Enthusiasm or the fire in the belly is something which IQ or academic rigour cannot compensate for. Enthusiasm is the derivate of passion-an unconditional love for something, some activity, or entity. Passion Quotient or PQ of an individual, therefore, becomes the game changer.

Transition through Ages—the Shifting Q's-BQ, IQ, EQ and PQ

As we moved along the ages, there was a gradual but conscious shift in the way human excellence was measured, or at least perceived.

Five to six hundred years ago, it was only the brute force that counted. The agricultural economy, with little technology available, demanded hard work on the fields. Wars were full of battle cries, backed by horses, catapults, spears, bows, arrows, and swords. Building forts, palaces, pyramids, and mansions, required thousands of slaves. Therefore, to survive, or to do well, it had to be the muscular might. Those were the days of brawn and not brain. Your performance and success, therefore, was directly proportional to the Brawn Quotient-BQ.

Then we shifted to the era of inventions and discoveries. The industrial economy boomed because of machines that did a lot more work and with lot less effort. Man became smarter as he used his brain to make machines which now worked for him. So our progress was measured with inventions and discoveries. In the first half of the twentieth century, there was a plethora of inventions and medicinal discoveries. These got us electricity, steam engine, cars, aircraft, and penicillin, to name a few. It was science alone that could solve the problem of hunger and poverty. Science and technology could generate jobs, provide comfort, and build economies. Industrial Revolution changed the shape of the world. Therefore, the basic disciplines like mathematics, physics, chemistry, and biology, became the pillars of excellence. Scientific approach was the new norm. Power shifted from your broad shoulders, to your head, and finally, to your brain. It was the era of inquiry, based on empirical and measurable evidence, subject to specific principles of logical reasoning.

There was, therefore, a need to test and benchmark human skills in this scientific and logical domain of reasoning. Human intelligence (or intellect) had to be scientifically measured for contextual scientific competence!

Scientists viewed human intelligence as one monolithic entity, which was based on a paper-pencil test known as an IQ test, a term coined by psychologist William Stern. Later, this was used as a predictor of job performance, educational excellence, income, and one's overall performance and well-being in the hierarchical society. This was the traditional definition of intelligence, based on cognitive aspects like problem solving, memory (retentivity), and receptivity.

Gradually, especially the post- Cold War period, saw a sudden shift in the way the economic development changed across the world. There was an increased importance of the service sector in the developed or industrialised economy. Developing countries saw the upswing in service-based products like, hospitality, airlines, retail, education, health, finance, IT, telecom, banking, etc. In addition, all products had a higher service component than in the first eight decades of the last century. In service economy, the concept of 'man behind the gun' becomes extremely important. Delivery of service depends more on the human being than a machine. Why do you choose X bank over a Y bank, or why do you prefer to fly by airline A and not B. A lot depends on the 'people' of that organisation. People, meaning their behaviours, their responses, do they care, are they prompt, are they polite, helpful, committed, and genuinely caring. Thus, there was again a shift of intelligence. Now, it shifted from the head to the heart, to finally, the emotions.

The term Emotional Intelligence was first used by Wayne Payne in his doctoral thesis, 'A study of Emotions: Emotional intelligence'. It got to the book shelves for people at large, with a book by Danial Goleman in 1995. Thus, began the realisation of the importance of Emotional Intelligence.

Globalisation, ICT, and the service sector economy has given rise to new opportunities. I am seeing this trend in business schools, where more and more students, instead of seeking jobs, are venturing into 'self-employment' and entrepreneurship. I see a definite shift from the existing few large organisations to small organisations coming up in large numbers, coupled with angel investors, venture capitalists, and banks backing 'ideas', which can make a viable business model. We are now moving from the information age to the entrepreneur age. This is now the new opportunity age. Number of jobs in monolithic organisations, could diminish, but the number of people seeking 'self-employment' in areas they love to work in, would be rapidly increasing, especially in the developing economies.

Here, I bring the aspect of 'love to work'. An entrepreneur or a self-seeker can perform optimally, if and only if he loves what he is getting into. This becomes a very critical point to ponder. You cannot start a venture and replicate success because some other fellow got into it and tasted success.

Fortunately, opportunities are so many, often limited only by our imagination, that one can always find something that one loves.

The next question is how does one find what ones loves? This is where passion chips in. This is what this book talks about, Passion Quotient—the ferocity with which you love to do something, and you cannot explain why.

The Young Turks

This book is for all age groups. But here, I am going to talk about those, who are getting into jobs, or are in B-schools. The most important question is, 'why business schools exist?' In most developing economies, most of the university graduates are not employable. Therefore, B-schools must lay stress on vocational aspects, rather than pure academics. We need people who can work and perform. I, therefore, view B-school curriculum as more vocational than educational. Here again, I would like to refer to the performance pyramid mentioned earlier. We do not require academically bright students for all the jobs that need to be filled. Every manager does not have to be a management scientist! Instead, we require willing horses and hardworking people, who value time and have 'reasonably sufficient' skills that a manager requires to perform effectively. We need effective managers and effective leaders who 'like' to perform.

We need such young Turks. For this, our education system— especially business schools, must create an 'environment to perform'. Culture defines environment, and we must focus on building a culture where people want to learn, display and practice what they feel that they are good at, identify, demonstrate, and live their passion. Student empowerment is best implemented in B-schools, where you have students in an age bracket of 20 to 30 years. Students are more mature and understand, to a large extent, their responsibility.

Passion and Profit Go Hand in Hand

If you look at profit as a by-product of passion, you will never go wrong. If you do what you love to do, then money will automatically follow.

As an author, over a period of time, I got several queries as to how profitable writing is. Some of these came as emails and a few during personal encounters with people. My answer to them is that, I write because I love to write and I do not focus on how much royalty my book is going to fetch. Imagine, before starting a painting, if a painter starts thinking how much will his work fetch him, or he says to himself, 'I will make a painting which will fetch at least half a million dollars', will he be able to put a price tag before he starts painting? Will he be able to concentrate on the painting with a 'price dagger' dangling over his head; the dagger which he himself has created?

One must expect some monetary returns, because passion does not mean charity. But if you do it for the love of it, you will never be disappointed with the money it would fetch you.

Books, Fantasy, and Passion

I am convinced that to sharpen your 'passion axe', reading books can help you greatly. Reading books opens up and widens mental horizons. Many times, it can indicate something you could not even imagine. It triggers your imagination, and hence, can trigger passion.

The book, 'Connect the Dots', narrates the story of M. Mahadevan, a university professor, and how he went on to become a successful hotelier. He was bitten by this 'hotelier bug' one day, when he was reading Arthur Hailey's book, 'Hotel'. Imagine, a passion which was so disconnected with his current profession and qualifications (he taught cost accounting), could be aroused, by reading a book, which beautifully portrays how a big hotel runs.

Mahadevan got his 'trigger', and then went on to work on it enthusiastically. Ultimately, he got his success.

Books make you fantasise; they portray a picture which is vivid, and many times larger than life. That is what fantasy is all about. Man fantasised to fly for hundreds of years, and one day, he flew.

Reading books on different subjects, especially fiction, can sometimes give you that direction which was buried or hidden within you for years. It can give life to a dormant passion, which, if left untouched, would go as utter waste. Reading biographies of successful people also motivates you, and often gives a direction to move on, to and explore new areas.

If you have already identified your passion, then read about those people, and their biographies, who have made it big in the same field. If you read at least three to four biographies of people who had a similar passion as yours, you will be able to understand how they went about their careers, and could make a success out of it.

You will not only get motivated, but will also be able to get a 'reality check', to what all difficulties they faced while pursuing their passion, and what all mistakes they made, which you should not make during your journey. You can also map your passion with those who have succeeded.

These personality studies will reflect as to what these guys have in them. More importantly, when you map your passion and your potential into such people's abilities, you get a clear picture of how passionate you are in actuality. It also makes you feel and learn what is out there, and is it for you or not.

I also observe that due to so much of media clutter, reading habits have taken a backseat. Book reading is one thing that can sharpen your intellect. In fact, it is like an addiction. Once you get hooked to it, it becomes a habit.

We at Excellence (**MILE**), make it a point that every post-graduate student reads one book in a month. These books range from short stories, fiction, mystery, and biographies.

Dream; but wake up

Fantasies, dreams, and a vision; all fall in one line. All those who dream to do something, are passionate at heart. Every one of us is a dreamer; each one of us likes to fantasise. That is why fantasy sells the most; in the form of books, as well as movies.

But dreams and fantasies alone get you nowhere. They must get translated into action. Remember the brief story of a professor who dreamt to become a hotelier I mentioned earlier. He began his dream by waking up. He started by moonlighting. He worked as a management trainee at a hotel in Chennai. During the day, he taught cost accountancy, and in the evening he worked as a 'night manager'. He would work for almost 18 hours a day. He neither compromised on his quality of teaching, nor did he change his evening duties. He could do this for three years, and without feeling any strain, because he loved what he did. In him, there was a fire to do well in life.

Passion is not restricted to doing specific things, or an 'activity' like, music, writing, a sport, or painting. This is also a revelation over the last five years. Now I feel it has a much larger scope. Passion to 'do well in life', is a new paradigm or a concept in the epistemological context. We have moved from the job-seeking age to the times when one can become a 'job giver'. Passion to be independent, passion to be your own master, passion to move away from the routine 9 to 5 job, is a reality today. Today, we are making more millionaires in a year than ever before, across the world. Age of opportunity, therefore, has redefined passion.

I would like to ring a warning bell here. While your passion may be to do well in life, but it is important to identify a field which you are comfortable with, in order to relaise your dream of doing well in life. It is better to do a 'test drive' at somebody else's cost, and see and feel how good the ride is. Mahadevan worked part time in a hotel, to understand the business, and to make up his mind (sub consciously though), whether he liked hotel business or not. Getting into something as serious as your profession, and changing tracks, could be disastrous without a test ride.

Autosuggestion to Propel Passion

Emil Coue, a pharmacologist, way back in 1880, used to leave a positive feedback with his patients about the medicine he gave them. He noticed that the patient to whom he praised about the efficacy of the medicine, had a notable improvement than those patients whom he had not mentioned anything. This was also later on known as the 'Placebo Effect'.

A derivative of this is the idea of Autosuggestion. Instead of someone suggesting, you suggest it to yourself! Using Autosuggestion or self-suggestion, one reaches the conscious mind, which in turn influences the subconscious mind. No thought or feeling can enter the subconscious mind without first entering the conscious mind through Autosuggestion. This could be a negative or a positive feeling, or a thought. A thought, therefore, generates a feeling. Similarly, a feeling generates a thought. In a way, the conscious mind serves as a guard for the subconscious mind. Therefore, nature has provided a mechanism to human beings, to have full control over our conscious mind. Many of us do not exercise this control, which can help us do better in life.

Napoleon Hill in his book, 'Think and Grow Rich', describes the use of Autosuggestion in a chapter on desire. If you read aloud several times daily, your desire for getting rich and also the feeling that you are already rich and have plenty of money, would set in your subconscious. Once you say this with full sincerity and emotions, you create thoughts which help you to achieve what you desire.

If you are passionate about something, then keep thinking about it all the time. Use Autosuggestion to say, 'I want to start my own business'. Define your business environment, feel it, see it, and soon, your passion will get converted into a viable career.

Fundamentally, success of Autosuggestion lies in emotions. Reading something aloud hundreds of times without emotions will be of no use at all. Therefore, for your passion to get embedded in your subconscious, you must mix your thoughts with emotions and feelings.

Remember, passion itself is a very strong emotion. Therefore, you are triggering an emotion with an emotion.

Ability to use Autosuggestion, effectively depends on your ability to concentrate upon your passion, which starts as your desire; your desire must get converted to a burning passion.

As they say 'First fake it, then make it'. In this case, you are faking it in front of your own mind, but with emotions and faith.

Do not Emulate Others, but Emulate Yourself

I earlier talked about reading biographies of those people who have been successful in the field that you wish to get into. They become your role models, you look up to them, and you want to be like them. Therefore, you study their behaviour, likes, dislikes, and strategies they applied to succeed. Such role models are very motivational for anyone, who seeks success. They become a guiding light for us, and also an inspiration.

At the end of the day, you must be yourself. You must get inspired, but do not imitate. There is a subtle difference between emulation and imitation. Imitation is downright copy.

The best way is to take the inspiration and move on. Do not emulate your role model, but carve a place for yourself, and rather emulate yourself; your real being, and what what you are from inside. This direct connect with yourself will help you grow and succeed.

A Push can Wake You Up

When we discuss passion, we largely focus on the self and looking inwards. We are supposed to realise it ourselves, as to what excites us, and what are our likes and dislikes.

But it may also happen that you never get a chance to explore what you like. For instance how can you comment about a dish unless you have tasted it? And how can you taste it if no one offers it to you in your entire lifetime? Sometimes you realise your strong affinity to something by chance or by accident. Let us say you have been into sales and marketing of industrial goods for almost a decade, which becomes your comfort zone, and you have never tasted anything outside of it. Then suddenly there is a recession in the manufacturing industry and a slump in the demand of industrial goods. You find yourself without a job. While looking for a job, you stumble upon an opportunity to get into real estate marketing, and you have no option but to take it because your mere survival is at stake. In other words, you have been pushed into a different domain, a zone where you have never been.

In a matter of months you may realise that, 'this is it' that you are good at. Therefore, many times, circumstances force us to change tracks, and could provide opportunities to find out what our passion is.

I strongly believe that in the area of education, our endeavour should be to expose students to different fields, which may be different from the core discipline. For instance, letting students of engineering, science, management, study, liberal arts and social sciences, is a breakaway idea. It gives students to look outside their cramped space, suffocated by a one-track approach. Such an exposure not only helps develop a rounded personality, but also lets the students realise, what stuff exists outside their domain. Some of them may get 'thought triggers' out of this for their next big thing, their passion.

I have done this experiment for the last several years, and I am happy to the extent that it gives my students a tremendous advantage in terms of handling competition in the job market.

Learning from Mistakes and Observation

Whatever technology, inventions, and development that we see around us, have taken thousands of years to build. Humans learnt by observation, by hit and trial, and by making mistakes. Over the lifetime of several generations in the past, millions of mistakes were made by individuals to create civilisations. Whether it was learning to bake an earthen pot in a hearth, or making a bridge over a river, all were learnt gradually, step-by-step, and never in one shot. Man probably learnt cooking when a piece of meat fell in a fire accidently, and later what was retrieved out of the fire was deliciously palatable.

People, who follow a dream, do not get it right the first time. They need to observe an act, and again observe if they are on the right path. This is so true for entrepreneurs. Reading many such stories, I have learnt that all those who follow their passion must be prepared to make a few mistakes. If you are not prepared, you may get disappointed and disheartened, which may deflate your enthusiasm.

Mistakes can be seen as experiments, while experiments can be seen as mistakes. Here, we play in the shades of grey, because there are no straight blacks or whites.

Idea of a Parallel Flame

During my long experience with young students who chose to undergo management studies, I have come across some students who have already excelled in a certain field.

One of my students, for example, had been into designing and making artificial jewellery. She has already established a small business, but was now looking at bigger prospects, and a career, after finishing the management programme.

There was another one who was a great photographer. His interest lay in photography, and he wanted to become a professional photographer. Not sure of the financial viability of this profession, he chose to do a management programme.

Yet another one was bitten by the 'lawyer' bug. This girl wanted to do management after acquiring a law degree. She could later open her own law firm. For this, the law bug must remain alive for the next several years, before she is ready to start her own venture.

In all these cases, one could see the Maslow's hierarchy of needs, coming into play. All three of them had a passion, but had to take a different direction, because of financial security, which became a barrier for them to take a plunge. What do you do in such a case? Were they to abandon forever what they loved? Was there a way out?

In many of my one-on-one sessions with students, some are very candid to tell me that they would ultimately start their own business, and want to make it big. Most are not clear about their roadmap, but are clear about the destination-'self-employment'.

My advice in such cases is very simple, 'Learn the discipline of management with me, and then manage your passion with this expertise under your belt. Most importantly, keep the parallel flame on.'

In this case, one takes a mid path. You are moving up, step-by-step, as per Maslow's hierarchy, and yet, not taking a plunge right away; you wait for the right time to make a switch from a corporate career, to follow your passion, and make a viable business or a career out of it.

One should sharpen the axe, learn the tricks of the trade, and develop business acumen, that will really help in optimising the impact of your passion.

For instance, this girl who was doing a small business out of making artificial jewellery, can make it really big once she learns to make a proper business plan, and raise finance for a nationwide launch of her brand of jewellery.

Love what You Hate

This is an important aspect of life, and very practical too. Many of us have our own little dreams, often connected to an activity that we love. You may nurse an aspiration to start an Italian restaurant, because you can cook very well, or you may be thinking of starting your own advertising company.

People fail to live their passion because of one fundamental flaw. 'They try to get into what they love, head on'. Majority of us do not have a financial backing of parents, and do not, therefore, have the luxury of doing what we want to do.

Hence, you may have to do odd jobs initially that are not in line with what you would ideally like to do. It could also happen that you may have to start from the lowest rung and gradually move up. This happens often in the film industry where, to get a foothold, is not easy. People start as assistants to great directors, and wait for their chance to make it big, one day. Remember, late M.F. Hussain started his career by painting large film posters and hoardings. He gradually moved to the art and craft domain, to create modern art paintings, which fetched him millions.

The wise guys accept, 'whatever comes their way', as long as it is somehow connected to their field of interest. They are prepared to do things that are neither pleasant, nor paying, because their ultimate goal is to make it big, in field that they love.

For a considerable time, you need to learn to love what you hate. I think this is the price one has to pay to follow ones heart, and ultimately become successful.

Do not Get Blinded by Money

I have seen people making professions out of their passions. Most of these turn out to be successful businesses, which actually started as a hobby. As times passes, the focus of a seemingly passionate person shifts from passion to the business. One gets bogged down so much with the day-to-day operations, that passion could fly out of the window. Most flawed cases are those who get blinded by money. The day you lose focus of your passion and focus entirely on money, that is the time when you could lose the game. It is therefore, good to make money, but never to lose focus and your passion, because that is what got you there.

Can Your Passion be of Use to Others or the Society at Large?

This is one question which needs to be answered in the affirmative, if your passion is meaningful. A common sense way of looking at it is that, 'how can something be useful to you when it is not of any use to anyone else?' It also lets you know your target audience. If the answer is yes, then who all does your passion help? And that is your target audience.

In case, for instance, your passion is public speaking and motivating others, then this quality of your helps a large number of people who need motivation and a direction in life. You can then decide to focus on college students or corporate executives, or both. At the end of it, this has to be a win-win situation for you as well as others.

Joy of giving is also a passion. People do charity from the bottom of their hearts. It helps the poor and needy, and it helps the giver in attaining peace and satisfaction.

Selling Your Dreams to Others

This becomes extremely important for people who work in organisations. Whatever be your job profile, you can still nurture a dream for yourself.

Technology guys aspire to devise some engineering marvel, or innovation, whereas, a marketing executive may have revolutionary ideas to market his product very differently.

Majority of the times one may not be in a commanding position to take a call to implement one's own ideas.

You have people in the hierarchy who take such decisions. It is very important to learn the art of selling your dream to your bosses, to get their approvals. You must be able to excite all the stakeholders to back your ideas.

This becomes a stumbling block for most people, as they cannot communicate their ideas to convince others.

There is no one thumb rule which can be used to convince others. But the best way is to think through and prepare a convincing argument. In addition, sound board it with your peers, and buy them in first, before pitching it to the decision makers. Once you and your peers are convinced, then follow it passionately to ensure that your idea gets approved and implemented. Remember, you require to passionately push for your passion.

Identify a Higher Purpose to Trigger Passion to Perform

To be proud is human; I feel pride in something that will motivate anyone. My experiment of dealing with students and also with men in uniform, has taught me that, linking pride to a job can motivate people more than anything else. Pride comes with a sense of purpose, 'why am I doing this?', must be answered honestly and with pure conviction.

For example, a scientist who is working on a life-saving drug, has a sense of purpose. I am assuming that the scientist is already passionate about research in the field of medicine. But the moment he is assigned a task which can save millions of lives in the future, he is catapulted to a different level of motivation and passion to perform.

Armed forces across the world remain motivated on a single factor of 'my country and honour'. For every soldier, there is a higher purpose: his country. This generates levels of passion which money can never generate. Most people join the uniformed service because of a sense of belonging, camaraderie, and sacrifice, for the sake of their country. Why someone would otherwise lay down his life for a salary of ₹ 30,000 per month. If organisation can identify a raison *de etre* (reason to exist) and project and propose this to its employees as a higher purpose convincingly, it will be easy to infuse passion in the people.

Professions where it becomes easy to connect with a higher purpose are healthcare, education, and even sports. Doctors see themselves as saviours, and teachers see themselves as game changers for their students. When you play for your nation at the Olympics, it gives a different high. Cricket players so passionately prepare and practice when they represent their respective countries. It is great to wear 'India' on your blazer!

Every business exists for some purpose; to fill an existing gap or void in the market. It is the duty of the top management and leadership to identify this purpose, and project it in a way that employees can relate to it as something meaningful, and something worth doing.

Making Organisations more Vibrant

This book is more about personal success, achievement, and above all, individual satisfaction. People who are successful individually, also contribute to the success of the organisation they work for. Therefore, it becomes imperative to motivate people and earn their loyalty.

One of the most important factors to make people work passionately for an organisation, is to build pride through the history of the organisation. Legacy has a great impact on individuals and gives a feeling, 'Oh, I work for a company which is a legend in itself'. Writings like 'Levis Strauss & Co. established 1873', or 'Chivas Regal established 1801', are quite common. It not only woos a customer, who gets a reassurance of a vintage brand, and therefore quality, but also gives a sense of pride to each and every employee.

This has been used very often and very successfully too in the armed forces. History of infantry battalions, and armoured regiments, are showcased to display valour and pride. This becomes a very important means to motivate the entire rank and file. People are prepared to lay down their lives for the honour of the battalion or regiment they belong to. This also builds camaraderie, lasting for generations. Customs and traditions in the armed forces may be found in the written form, or could pass down the years as unwritten laws. Men in uniform observe these traditions and uphold them as a matter of pride, and take them seriously, as these keep them mindful of the heritage of their corps, or their service. For instance, the Japanese military tradition was based on the Bushido Code. It meant 'the way of a warrior', and was analogous to chivalry. It was a tradition stressing on loyalty, frugality, and honour, unto death.

Traditions are also a part of culture, and responsible for building pride, and a sense of belonging. If an employee is not really passionate about his work profile, he can become an enthusiastic employee who takes pride in working for his company.

These traditions are built over a period of time, but act as a beacon or a guiding spirit for employees to let them know 'The way things are seen and done here'. Legends often become the role models, and traditions are created or come into being according to their behaviour. This organisational tradition defines the values, norms, and beliefs of the organisation. In fact, traditions transform an organisation from the brick and mortar shell to a living organism.

In the new economy, most of the organisations are very young. They have no legacy to talk about. Many such organisations were the result of the entrepreneur's era, which we have been witnessing since the last couple of decades. What can they talk about? I feel such organisations must talk about speed at which they grew, as many of them do grow at a very rapid pace. They can also talk about the new business space they created for themselves. Usually, entrepreneurs themselves are very enthusiastic, and since their organisations are relatively small, their passion can easily rub off on their employees. They can themselves become role models for their employees, and can coin their own trademark statements.

Mark Zuckerberg at the age of 20, created facebook, a social networking service in February 2004, and by October 2012, had one billion active users, a revenue of around four billion American dollars. His story can motivate every employee of the company.

Thomas J. Watson, the founder of IBM had 'Think' as his trademark motivational word. This one word was placed prominently one wall of every room. Every employee carried a notebook called 'Think', and the entire stationary carried this word. Not surprisingly then, IBM has now come up with the IBM ThinkPad.

Stories about founders and great achievers act as triggers to motivate people. At the same time, many employees can identify their own passion with such people. Henry Ford, the Founder of Ford Motors, was an inspiration for many. His focus was mass production, reduced cost, but high wages for his employees. A term 'Fordism', was coined to depict this philosophy, and his commitment to optimise production to lower costs, resulted in many business and technical innovations.

Looking at the recent success stories, Google and Facebook would make great inspirational reading. Many passions could get (I am sure would have) triggered by stories of such young turks and their meteoric rise.

Passion, Vision, Mission

I would have read hundreds of vision and mission statements of organisations, which are into hospitality, health, aviation, manufacturing, education, and even entertainment. Most of these look very idealistic, often devoid of any clear purpose.

Passion and purpose are closely-related entities because, you have to be first convinced about something (its purpose) before you develop a passion for it. As a corollary, I find most of the vision and mission statements lacking passion. Mission is a strongly felt calling, and so is passion.

So whenever you sit down and write your vision and mission, statements, align them to your passion, and you will be bang on target.

If the top management of an organisation is passionate about their mission, there is no doubt that the organisation will do extremely well in whatever they have decided to do.

Accreditations, Recognitions, Ranking, and Certifications

Do accreditations and certifications factor in the organisational passion? Let me explain this. There are hundreds if not thousands of professional accreditations for organisations operating in different business domains. Accreditation process is very scientific and structured, often based entirely on evidence or documentary recordings/proofs. These rules and processes apply uniformly to each and every organisation that seeks accreditation, which normally (in most cases) results in the award of a grade.

These processes are very cut and dry, and synthetic in nature. They have to be, to avoid any human bias in the assessment. They are designed to be objective, so that subjectivity does not creep in. It simply means that there is no room for emotions in such assessments.

It also implies that the softer aspect, the emotional intelligence and passion of the organisation, are not taken into account.

An organisation consists of hardware and software. The hardware part consists of the brick and mortar, the infrastructure, the machinery, etc. People are the software. Brick and mortar does not have a heart or emotions, but people do.

I must reiterate that, in the service sector, this aspect becomes much more relevant than it was in the industrial economy era.

People are the integral part of an organisation, and I feel very strongly that the EQ and PQ of an organisation must be kept in mind, while grading or assessing any organisation. It sounds abstract, but a thought must go into this aspect. In future, a serious study needs to be undertaken, in order to quantify this unquantifiable thought.

Let me take education as an example. Evaluation of an educational institution is done based on several factors. Predominantly, the infrastructure and facilities form one major input, and second one is the quality of the faculty, which is based entirely on their qualifications. In most cases, the admission cut-offs are also taken into considerations.

But all these are facts and figures, and do not account for passion, enthusiasm, or the emotional acumen of the people—students as well as the faculty.

To simplify, EQ of an organisation (which is determined by its environment), is linked to the EQ strengths of the leader or the top leadership, comprising of top-level executives. This has been established and indicated by several studies, including the one cited by Daniel Goleman. If the top leadership is enthusiastic and high on EQ, it will directly and positively impact the organisational effectiveness, through its positive culture, set by the top leadership. Same thing is applicable to PQ. If the top brass is passionate about their vision and mission, the rest of the organisation will follow.

Therefore, it boils down to the fact that assessment of an organisation must take into account the passion quotient of the top leadership.

It may not be, and is not possible to quantify it, but so is the case for culture. Both these are interlinked, and I feel the assessing team, while having a one-on-one session with the top leadership and a few employees, must try to 'feel' the level of passion they have. They need to device their own methods/tools to arrive at some conclusion. It may not get reflected as a number, but can always find a place in the pen picture or remarks, when assessments, and reports are prepared. Maybe some more research in the future will be able to peg the PQ of an organisation to a number or a grade.

Best practices of an organisation, especially those which are unique, can be an indicator of organisational passion and enthusiasm. New experiments are steps toward creativity, and hence, must not be ignored. Even if experiments have failed, they must be given some credit, as they indicate the passion to do something different. Today, the best practices are taken into account for assessing and grading organisations. I feel more weightage should be given to these.

Passion at Work

Passion and purpose go hand in hand. I have put my bet on this fact in a couple of my earlier books. In my books, I am going to clearly establish that, 'the rich and the famous, the movers and the shakers are not necessarily high school toppers'. In the last few years, especially after I founded a business school of my own, I have been able to aggressively pursue this belief. My experiment with this truth has helped me in proving my hypothesis right.

At MILE, we select students who may be just average in their academic performance, but have a 'desire' to do well in life, and are prepared to work for it.

One must cater for the fact that there can be several reasons for an individual to perform poorly in the academic domain. It could be lack of direction, bad environment, no parental guidance, bad school, underperforming UG college, and above all, an academic environment, which does not even challenge a student to put in hard work.

We at MILE proudly say, that 'we take ordinary students and make them perform extraordinarily'. The mantra for success at MILE is to 'challenge' every student to put in his or her best. Create an environment of excellence, so that every student puts in his or her best. Build enough rigour in the programme, so that the lowest denominator also starts putting in his or her best efforts. Over the first semester, you change the attitude of every individual towards individual excellence and energy. In the second semester, one sees a big change in every individual. Most of the students by now, realise what is their actual cup of tea, and that is the first step to move towards finding their passion. Sometimes you need to be pushed to seek your passion. This is not easy. It required a very planned, organised, and dedicated efforts from every member of the management team, and all the faculty members.

If a similar effort is made at an undergraduate level, one could witness a tremendous improvement in the national asset in terms of human resource.

This book has been translated in several Indian regional languages. The tipping point of its acceptability came with a Vietnamese publisher, approaching me to ask for translation rights in Vietnamese. I am glad that now this book is available in Vietnamese language as well.

Passion, over Enthusiasm, and Restraint

This is something I have again realised in the last few years. If you are overly passionate, you could go grossly wrong. For creative people like writers, painters, or film-makers, this is very important. It has been often observed that an artist in his enthusiasm may cross certain societal boundaries, which could harm him in the long run. A painting or a film could hurt the sentiments of a particular faith or a community. It is imperative that every creative person keeps this in mind while executing his project.

For those venturing out into new business areas, over enthusiasm or too much of passion could cloud their judgment or sometimes make them blind. Such business ventures could ultimately results in entrepreneur's trap.

Therefore, while it is good to listen to your heart (passion), it is also important to keep the windows of your mind (reason) open, when attempting something new.

Another interesting observation is that, once a person is passionate about something he/she wants to do, or something he/she wants to create, people around hem/her hesitate telling him/her the truth. Their peers, juniors, and even seniors, may not advice them correctly, in order not to hurt them. This harms more than it helps. A candid feedback may sound harsh, but it is worth a lot, as it can save huge embarrassment or even financial losses in the future.

Today, media has not only become alert, but has also become very aggressive. Reporters and news channels look for opportunities to make news. An artist, a painter, a movie maker, or a writer, is a sitting duck. If one does not exercise self-restrain or self-censoring, one can come under media glare very easily. Social activists are also in fashion today, and tend to point fingers at the drop of a hat at anything they see as unacceptable to them. At the same time, I feel very strongly that creative people must use their right to exercise freedom of speech and expression. But keep this cardinal principle in mind that, 'being transparent does not mean being naked!' And you will never go wrong in your creative judgment.

Another aspect of being too passionate is that, one becomes too focused. Being too focused implies a narrowed path of thinking. In the world of opportunities, one can miss out many avenues, if one gets obsessed about one particular idea.

Creativity and Passion-A Relook

I have devoted one full chapter to creative competence, where I derived a strong link between creativity and passion, which is, 'passionate people are creative'.

We need to examine yet another aspect of creativity, which is not linked to passion; in fact, it is quite the opposite of passion.

An agitated mind cannot produce creative thoughts. Therefore, anxiety, fear, high stress levels, and fear of failure/criticism, can become creative blockers. A calm and composed mind delivers the optimum creative output.

Meditation of any form aims at lowering the agitativity of mind. Whether it is Transcendental Meditation (TM) or it is Vipassana, the methods may differ, but all of them endeavour to create an equanimous mind, a calm mind, a mind which is at ease with itself. Studies and experiments show that meditation helps increase creative thinking of an individual.

Meditation may not make you a creative genius, but definitely will put you in a better position to think clearly, form original insights, and approach problems from new directions.

Cahn and Polich studied the effect of meditation on the brain. They employed neuroimaging techniques to hundreds of people. They came to the conclusion that those who practiced meditation or TM had considerably more blood flow to cerebral cortex during meditation. This indicated that the mind reaches the fourth state of consciousness. It, thus, induces the stage 1 sleeper or the twilight stage, without inducing drowsiness. Mind is very calm but yet very alert, which is the best possible state for a mind to be creative.

While conventional sleep decreases blood flow in the brain, meditation increases the flow of blood. With more and more practice, meditation induces deeper and deeper sleep, yet retaining high level of consciousness and awareness.

Passion and Human Brain

In the earlier edition, I had not touched upon this aspect related to passion. I feel that a brief description of anatomy of human brain in the context of passion will help the readers to understand the complexity of human emotions.

During the evolution of mankind, the human brain developed gradually, and in a phased manner. As would be obvious, the primitive brain developed first, and its purpose was self-preservation (reptilian brain). Over and above, this developed the limbic system (old mammalian brain) which was the seat of emotions. Much later, enveloping the limbic system, the rational brain known as neo cortex (new mammalian brain), gradually developed, which was for rational and intellectual tasks.

Passion, being a strong emotion, originates from the limbic system, which itself is a complex structure, consisting of three main substructures, thalamus, hypothalamus, and amygdala. These all are inter-connected, and none of them may be connected to any specific emotional state, which are huge in number, and vary in their range substantially.

Limbic system as a whole is responsible for all our emotions. The health of this system determines our behaviour, emotions, and well-being.

It is the center of our spiritual awakening, social life, and emotional life responses. This part of the brain provides us the emotional juices, and is responsible for our feelings, both negative as well as positive. We experience the passion and desire to move forward in life because of the limbic system.

When limbic system gets into an overactive mode, negative thoughts take over, and passion goes out of the window, leading to lack of enthusiasm. Depression and lethargy are also associated with this.

Limbic system affects the autonomic (which acts involuntarily) nervous system, and the endocrine system. The autonomic nervous system affects digestion, salivation, perspiration, and even heart rate. All these, as we know, get affected by our state of mind. This system gets affected by recreational drugs such as alcohol, caffeine, and nicotine and also drugs which are in the narcotic list of substances.

People use these mind altering substances to stimulate the limbic system and derive an 'artificial high' for themselves. That is why intoxication has been called as the 'Fourth drive' by psychopharmacologists, stating that human instinct to take recreational drugs is comparable to satisfying hunger, need for shelter, or thirst.

Passion-The Sixth Level of Maslow's Hierarchy of Needs

In a paper 'Theory of Human Motivation', Abraham Maslow described the hierarchy for human needs; this theory was later explained fully in his book *Motivation and Personality*.

This theory describes the five layers or levels of needs a human being attempts to satisfy in an hierarchical way. At the bottom of this hierarchy (sometimes depicted as a pyramid) is the need for meeting the physiological needs of a human being. These are the essentials for survival, like food, water, shelter, and even breathing. These needs having been met, a human being looks at other needs like security, sense of belonging, and self-esteem; in this order. These are also known as deficiency needs. As long as these layers or any one of them is deficient (or not met) there is no desire to move to the next level, the fifth level of self-actualisation.

The term self-actualisation has been perceived differently by different psychologists. Kurt Goldstein, a German Jewish neurologist, a and a psychiatrist, defined it as a motivation to realise or fulfill one's full potential, and to exploit one's full potential, or to activate all the capacities that one has.

Maslow, in his hierarchy of needs, states that the fifth and final state of self-actualisation can be achieved only when the first four basic needs have been fulfilled. Obviously, you cannot do your best or deliver your optimum, unless you have sufficient food to eat, have security and shelter, friends and family, and have your esteem and respect among the society. In modern societies and in the advanced/developed countries, these four needs are met or have been usually met for all citizens, and they, if desired, can move to the level of self-actualisation.

The quotation 'What a man can be, he must be', very well explains what self-actualisation actually means; it is the desire to accomplish and achieve everything that one can. This level of need (as stated by Maslow or as perceived by him) can only arise once the previous levels of achievements have been fully achieved. In the first edition of this book, I had written about this aspect, and had positioned passion as the self-actualisation stage of an individual's being. Having discussed this with many individuals, and how they manage to short circuit some of the intermediatory states, and reached the self-actualisation much sooner, I had to reposition passion as a stage beyond the fifth level of Maslow's Hierarchy.

Living your passion can be positioned beyond self-actualisation, because it is not necessary for you to live by your passion, only after the first four levels of needs have been met. Passion, in fact, gives you that kind of motivation, that, even if you are not earning a decent living, you can live by your passion. All the five levels and the desire to fulfill the need as defined by Maslow, are driven by the rational mind, and are not emotionally driven for an individual. That is why these are achieved sequentially. It is very logical that unless a human being has food and shelter, he will not be able to think of self-esteem or have a sense of belonging. He has to fill up his stomach first, before he can think of anything else.

The need to do something due to your passion, is emotionally-driven, and hence, it is possible for someone to do without even meeting a need at a lower level of the hierarchy and move beyond self-actualisation.

Therefore, passion lets you break these hierarchical barriers, and achieve something spectacularly satisfying, because you do not care for the lower levels. For example, a passionate singer or a musician can pursue his/her passion for the art, as long food and shelter are taken care of. Artists do not long for job security or a sense of belonging. For them, the biggest driver and satisfaction is their love for music. This is very prevalent in film, art, and drama, and even in sports.

And once you reach the sixth level, a level beyond self-actualisation, the self-actualisation is already achieved. This state is the state of Nirvana, where you feel liberated. That is why the job profile becomes very important, especially in senior positions. People are prepared to relocate, and may not worry so much about the compensation or salary, as long as they love their job; and if passionate, so much better.

If one examines this aspect critically, in many cases, level five and six would have some overlap. Many people who seek to fulfill their passion, say post-retirement for instance, will do it only after the first four levels have been taken care of.

They are not madly passionate, and hence, go logically, level after level, and decide to achieve the ultimate goal, when they are in their comfort zone, economically, and in every other way.

Is Passion an Intelligence?

As early as 1983, Howard Gardner in his book *Frames of Mind* laid the foundation of multiple intelligence theory. His basic premise was that, around 1960, there was a virtual absence of any mention of the arts in major text books. The focus was only on the scientific thinking. His goal was to find a suitable place for arts in the academic domain, and also in psychology. He defined seven types of intelligences in great detail. For any human ability to qualify as an intelligence, he also came up with the right 'signs' of an intelligence or specific indicators. This was a set of criteria that could qualify something as intelligence. He also mentions something very interesting about the options he had in front of him—whether to call it intelligences or faculties, or sundry gifts or abilities or talents. He chose 'intelligence', and this minor lexiconal substitution made people sit up and take a note of it.

In my book, *The Winning Edge-Decoding the power within* I divide these seven intelligences into three blobs of excellence.

1. Linguistic intelligence, logical, and mathematical intelligence put together, makes the IQ blob.

2. Spatial Intelligence, kinesthetic intelligence, and musical intelligence, make for the 'gifted' blob. I call it the gifted blob because, music, art and sports to a large extent, are gifted abilities.

3. Interpersonal intelligence and intrapersonal intelligence is the EI blob or the emotional intelligence blob. This, in fact, is a 'supportive' intelligence, as it supports the first two.

For instance, if you have a potential to sing, and possess a great idea of rhythm as well as beat, you can be destined to be a great singer. But this will happen only if you have the drive, determination, and dedication (all three fall in the EI blob); without these, you may not be able to become a playback singer.

Similarly, even if you are good at mathematics and logic, you will not be able to crack a competitive examination, unless you diligently prepare for it.

Gardner in his book does not put a cap or a limit on the number of intelligences which, as per his analysis, are only seven. In fact, the realisation of EI came much after the multiple intelligence theory of Gardner. EI theory has intangibles like 'social intelligence'—the ability to understand feelings of people. This becomes very important in the context of a service-based economy, where people management became very important. Managing, retaining, and training people became one of the most important business imperatives.

Gardner has established certain prerequisites of intelligence, and tries to establish what intelligence is after all. He first says that, 'it must enable an individual to resolve genuine problems or difficulties, or create effective products'. Then he says that the prerequisites are a way of ensuring that a human intelligence must be 'genuinely useful and important'—at least in certain cultural settings. To illustrate this point, he takes the ability of individuals to recognise faces, and to argue that this cannot be taken as an intelligence. He discards the ability to 'recognise faces' as an intelligence, because it was not valued by cultures. In simple words, it is not of any use, nor is it productive for humanity.

Going by this argument, I would say that reverse should also be true, which means 'any ability' which can be of any use to an individual, in the context of a culture, should qualify as an intelligence.

Today, in the context of free economy, passion is the most important success parameter. Going into details and mapping 'passion' into the eight 'signs' or indicators of intelligence that Gardner came up with for a human ability to be termed as intelligence, I am of the firm opinion that passion qualifies to be termed as a definite human intelligence. It does meet most of the parameters given in the set of criteria by Gardner. Some of the 'signs' are only just indicators, and Gardner very nicely puts it as 'this is an area where speculation is tempting and firm facts especially elusive'. Passion is a part of the EI blob, but separately stands out as an effective enabler for success, and hence, is one of the very important human sundry gift or intelligence.

Passion, in addition, is a catalyst or an augmenter for all human abilities. It is supportive in nature, and can enhance human performance beyond one's expectations. Passion is not only intelligence, but is also an emotion. As Plato wrote, around 2,000 years ago, 'all learnings have an emotional base.' Passion definitely matters a lot in the context of human learning and success.

PQ Test

There are standard tests for IQ which have been in existence for almost a century. EQ tests are far more recent, and yet, not standardised. The reason could be that the Emotional Intelligence is not very amenable to being quantified.

Mayer-Salovey-Caruso Emotional Intelligence Test (MSCEIT) is based on Mayer and Salovey model of EI. It is based on emotion-based problem appreciation and solution. It tests a person on all four abilities or domains of EI. It gives a score for each domain, and also a total score. It is taken as an ability test, but it is not like an IQ test, because the questions do not have objectively correct responses. It has more than hundred questions, but the correlation between the test result and how much emotionally intelligent that person is perceived by his peers and subordinates, is not very encouraging. In addition, there are other tests like Bar-on model of Emotional Social Intelligence. The test is a measure of emotional and social behaviour, and gives an estimate of one's emotional and social intelligence. It is a way of gauging the ability of an individual in the context of his dealing with the environment, people, challenges, and pressure. People can fake and score better results, and hence, this test is not very robust.

There has been very little or virtually no effort to create a PQ test. Since passion is an ability to enhance success and performance in a particular domain, and I see it as an intelligence, I have created a test for estimating an individual's passion for a particular thing, activity, or desire.

At this stage, this can give a broad indication to the person who takes the test, as to how passionate he 'actually is' for something he 'feels' he is passionate about. Scores would be only indicative. I feel, for a person taking this test, more important would be to revisit the attempted answers, and get some broad directions to understand how passionate he/she is, and what can they do to improve.

The Road Ahead

I feel a lot more needs to be formulated in the cultural context. How to generate passion in schools and educational domain is a very huge area for research. Measuring passion and its practical interpretation is yet another area where a deeper study is required. The test that I have created needs to be validated and gradually improved upon. Last but not the least, a means to enhance individual passion needs to be discovered. We need to develop some tools and tutorials to enhance passion in people. A lot can be done in the area of creativity and passion—as both of these are closely connected. This can be a game changer in the human competence domain in the long run.

Virender Kapoor

2014

What Do You Think Passion is?

That Fire in the Belly

The most powerful weapon on earth is the human soul on fire.

- Field Marshal Ferdinand Foch

What Is Passion?

If I ask a simple question, 'What colour do you like? Red, green, or blue?' The answer could well be 'well I love blue!' If I ask you, 'Why do you love blue?' you may not have an answer and you would most likely say, 'I just love blue, what is your problem'. 'What about red?' you say 'Yuck ... I hate it.' So there it is – we like some colours and we hate some of them, and we have no particular reasons for these likes and dislikes. You love it so you love it, and you hate it so you hate it, that's it.

Passion also works on similar lines. There are certain things which are close to our hearts and we just love doing them; we are supposed to be passionate about these things. We have no reasons or no logical explanations for this affinity. And that in simple words is Passion.

Whenever I get to a low point, I go back to the basics. I ask myself 'why am I doing this ?' It comes down to passion.

– Lynst James

You hate red – right? What about some colour combinations and variations. If I can be creative and use some other shades, and combine them with red to create some patterns, chances are that you would like them. You may not like to wear red trousers, but you would love to drive a blazing red Ferrari! Ok, look at the Nazi flag – the famous third Reich flags – red background, white circle in the middle, and a black swastika! Looked powerful and mesmerising. You may now love the red in it. Have you seen the recent Airtel logo? It also uses red, white, and black colours creatively, and it looks amazing. So you may like some colours and hate some of them in isolation, but you may change your opinion when you mix and match these colours.

And let me tell you, your choice of colours also changes with time. As you grow up or mature, you may not like a 'shocking blue' or a 'shocking pink'. You may start liking pale pastel pinks, or pale yellows with white and aqua blue! As we react to colours, we also react to our jobs, interests, hobbies, and almost all our activities. These reactions and likes or dislikes also change with time. As we can creatively mix colours and start liking those which we hated when we saw them individually, we can well make changes in our activities at home and office, to make things more interesting.

If you look at successful people, they love what they do. There are people who love to win, and love to achieve. If achievement gives you a high, achievement is your stimulant. Many students love to see their name on the role of honour, nailed high up on the wall in the college, and that target becomes their passion. Then they work to achieve it. Actors like Shah Rukh Khan love to act and love to win. In many of his interviews he said that, 'I love to receive awards'. Thus, to receive public appreciation and appreciation of the jury, he puts in his best, and that is his passion.

In fact it is your very soul, what you love to do, what amuses you, pleases you, and excites you spontaneously. Nature has strange ways of putting us on the right track. Fear is a basic instinct, so that we, in times of danger, – can react to protect ourselves.

> Success is not the result of spontaneous combustion, you must set yourself on fire.
>
> – *Reggie Leach*

In the same way, passion has been put into us by nature, so that we can know when we are on the right track or are on target. This enables us to chase things that we are capable of. This acts like an inner compass or a guiding light. It shows you the direction and also gives you the necessary push to reach your target. In this case, the target in fact pulls you or attracts you, and you really don't feel that you are pushing yourself. That's the beauty of being passionate about something. Look at Aamir Khan – as an actor to give a perfect shot is what is his passion, or maybe competing with himself is his passion. He doesn't get tired of giving the same shot hundred times over, till he can say to himself that it was perfect.

Passion does two things for us: first, it drives us to be ourselves and live and behave like what we actually are. Second, it also means being in harmony or integrity with ourselves. If you want to be more than ordinary, passion is the key. If you want to be one of those 'who also ran the race...' then you can well do without it. In the military parlance they say, 'Morale is nothing but the state of mind'. If morale is the state of mind, then I would like to say that, 'Passion is nothing but the state of the heart'.

It has more to do with chemistry than physics. It has to be the adrenalin flowing in your blood, more than anything else. Now let us examine what it does to an individual. How does it affect our being. It could evoke different emotional states in us, and also be present in different forms.

Different Colours of Passion

Passion shows. You can feel it in different forms and colours. Let us look at some of its colours and forms:

• Passion is Your Soul – An Inner Calling

Gautam Buddha was an extraordinary, yet an ordinary human being. It was his inner calling that moved him on in the search of peace; this quest for enlightenment was actually bound to love and compassion for others. He was aware of the fact that if he himself was bound to attachments and cravings, then the whole lot of humanity must also be bound in the same way. This inner calling motivated him to renunciate his family and kingdom to find a way out for the humanity, from prevailing miseries and aversions. This would be the highest form of passion, and if present or invoked, can influence people to make great sacrifices, and turn ordinary people into extraordinary human beings.

• Passion is a Source of Tremendous Energy

Most energetic people are passionate. A wrestler or a boxer may have a lot of power in his punches, but it requires a different type of energy to move that power. Remember Cassius Clay or Muhammad Ali – 'who moved like a butterfly and stinged like a bee'? Muhammad Ali's story of how he became a boxer goes something like this. At the age of 12 in 1954, his bike got stolen and he was very upset. While he was fuming to teach the thief a lesson, a cop told him, 'you better learn to box first', which he did, and within weeks, he won his first bout. For the next three decades, he would be in the ring, and became the world heavy weight boxing champion in 1964 –, all in 10 years. The key to success for Cassius Clay was 'passion for excellence', which gave him courage and inculcated in him strict personal discipline and dedication. Obviously, he had tremendous unmatched energy levels.

Bruce Lee became a Hollywood legend because of his passion-driven dedication to cull out a shapely body which the world envied. His love for martial arts was unmatchable. A poor boy from Hong Kong becomes world's most famous movie icon having as much impact as may be Elvis Presley, Merlyn Monroe and James Dean. More than a phenomenon, Jackie Chan is a one-man industry who writes, directs, and acts in his films. He lives and breathes films, and once you see him on the sets, he is always like a fireball – full of enthusiasm, energy, and passion for his work.

Co–stars of Shah Rukh Khan often say that, 'This man has tremendous energy – he is like a power house'. He may not have the strength of Bruce Lee or Cassius Clay, but has tremendous amount of energy, because he loves cinema.

If you are passionate about something, then at the end of it, it has to satisfy you. Sanjeev Kapoor of the Khana Khazana fame quips, 'When you prepare food with love, affection and passion, it exceeds expectations'. Once a meal is cooked the chef gets a tremendous sense of satisfaction. Similarly, a good mechanic who loves his job and does it with enthusiasm, finds a sense of satisfaction after he tunes in a car or a bike.

• State of Excitement – Passion gives that High

Sometimes one wonders why people fly fighter aircrafts on March 2, and Mach 2 and risk their lives doing all sorts of aerobatics. Fighter pilots in the Indian Air Force are paid much lesser for flying the Sukhoi aircraft, than commercial pilots flying Boeings. But the kick which these young pilots get out of flying a sleek fighter plane, is much more than flying anything else. I have seen fighter pilots who have been grounded for medical reasons, going almost into a state of clinical depression, because the opportunity to fly has been snatched away from them. When a pilot pulls an aircraft into a loop, the gravitational force acting on him literally drains the blood out of his head. It is physically very strenuous and drains energy out of you. Moreover, the casualty rate amongst fighter pilots is very high as compared to any other profession. Almost all fighter pilots – despite the risk fly because they love to fly. They fly because it gives them a high.

• Passion Attracts You

Smell of oil paint and the feel of a taut canvas on a frame gets the blood running in any artist's veins. It really beckons him to splash the paint. Good music would always set John Travoltas, Madonna's, and Michael Jackson's foot tapping.

I love music and play more than one musical instrument. I love playing the drums, and when I see a band playing some song, I always feel like getting on to the stage, and to play with the group. I have done this on many occasions, and I simply love it.

• Passion is Something for which You Care

You become passionate about something when it touches your heart, your very core. I have a friend, whose wife works for an organisation that looks after people who are suffering from AIDS. She has to travel a lot, many a times to the interiors of rural areas, and it is a very demanding work. Since it is run by an NGO, the monetary rewards are far from satisfactory. Yet, I find her very enthusiastic about her work.

Margaret Giannini's story is very inspiring. She was an attending physician at a medical school, doing her job perfectly well as any of her colleagues, till one day she had a chance to meet five couples who were the parents of mentally challenged children. They were unable to find a medical facility to treat their children, because none existed for such children. They felt humiliated and exasperated. They told their touching stories and experiences to her, and she was shocked to learn that such an attitude existed within the medical fraternity.

She was deeply touched, and just to help them, she started one morning, a week-clinic for their children. This simple decision which came straight from her heart changed her life. She soon became the founder of the first and the only clinic of its kind in the world, tending to the physical needs of mentally challenged children. She eventually decided to commit herself to the plight of these people.

In 1979, she was appointed as the first director of National Institute of Handicapped Research (NIHR) by Jimmy Carter, the then president of the US. Later, she was appointed principal deputy assistant secretary for Aging by President, George W Bush, and then rose to be the director of Health and Human Services office.

This is the story of passion, which got kindled because something- place in the same line.

• Visualising Passion

Seeing yourself being there, or seeing the end product, is also a shade of passion. Great sportsmen visualise themselves standing on the victory stand, the thunderous applause of the audience, and the chief guest handing over the trophy. It's all in the mind. The power and clarity of this vision which is produced by passion gives energy to these champions. These guys can see what they want to achieve. The clarity of the end result could well define the power of passion that you possess. Great architects, car designers, and fashion designers, have that end-product in front of their eyes – a beautiful Gothic architecture, a sleek sports car, or a beautiful dress – and that is passion.

• Passion can Make You Walk that Extra Mile

You don't feel the effort. If gardening is what you love, you don't mind watering the plants or taking out the weeds, even if it is very hot in the afternoon.

'I can walk that extra mile just for a Camel!' Remember this punch line for Camel cigarettes? Smoking is addictive, and so is passion. It will prod you to walk that extra mile, and you will, at the end of it, not even feel that you have put in any extra effort. We can perform certain activities without even feeling the effort. If any activity appears to be effortless, then it is a strong indicator that it could be your passion.

At the National Defence Academy, the training schedule is very rigorous and demanding. People look forward to a term break, when they can go home for a month and relax. During these holidays or the break period, the Mountaineering Club at the Defence Academy organises expeditions. Those who volunteer for these expeditions have to forgo the term break, miss a chance to go home and meet their parents, and go for the expedition. I have seen great amount of enthusiasm amongst these mountaineers who willingly go in for these expeditions during the term break, while their colleagues and friends relax at home. After the expedition they join the training scheduled for the next term, without even getting a single day break! For them, climbing mountains is a break, and they don't mind doing it at all – in fact, they enjoy it.

• Passion is Ecstasy and Love

> Essentially, the New York Philharmonic is just like any other orchestra — they all have the spirit of kids, and if you scratch away a little of the fatigue and cynicism, out comes a 17 year old music student again, full of wonder, exuberance, and a tremendous love of music.
>
> *– Zubin Mehta*

When you see music conductors of the genre of Zubin Mehta, stand on the stage and conduct a show, you see a man in ecstasy. He is one hundred per cent involved in what he is doing. Such people are, as if possessed by something. You cannot reach such heights of human excellence unless you have tremendous love for what you do. You would find the same state of ecstasy in case of great tennis players, golfers like Tiger Woods, or actors of the class of Amitabh Bachchan. In one of the popular shows 'Koffee with Karan', anchored by Karan Johar, the famous Bollywood actor, Amitabh Bachchan was asked the secret of success, or how he can deliver such intense performances. He said something very simple yet important. He said, 'when I go in front of the camera, I don't know something happens to me, and I just automatically perform'. This is a state of flow, total joy, or ecstasy, coming straight from the heart.

• Passion for Something

I play drums because I love playing music, I love the sound of it, I love playing in a group when there are three or more guitarist and somebody playing the saxophone or a keyboard! I play with an amateur band for hours, and for free. When you are prepared to do something for free, then it is a strong indication that your heart is into it, and you are passionate about it.

Taking the example of Shah Rukh Khan again, he says, that I am prepared to work for free if the role is good and that, being in front of the camera is for the love of it. Whereas, doing ads makes up for the money. The activity which you are prepared to do even if you have comfortable income flowing from other means, is a strong indicator of passion.

No one can change the world who isn't obsessed.

– Billie Jean King

Passion and Obsession

Obsession is a step beyond passion. Obsession is when you are so much in love with it, that you lose your balance of mind – so much so that, it gets the better of you. In fact, there is a very thin dividing line between the two. It is not unusual finding enthusiastic people being obsessive sometimes. Obsession in a way has a negative connotation, where you lose your sense of balance, and even well-being. It may become a pain for others and it could also be harmful for the individual himself. When Obsession reaches the state of mental spasm, it can be dangerous.

Most of the time, the line between the two is blurred, and you will often see enthusiastic people flip flopping between being passionate and obsessive. As long as you can keep your feet firmly on the ground, and keep your head cool and levelled, it is fine to be obsessive at times. Achievers often do this.

People with passion, in general, are enthusiastic, energetic, ready to go, and most importantly, very involved. They have that fire in the belly which makes them perform better than others. Many a times, some of these people demonstrate affinity for specific things bordering obsession. Out of hundred people you meet, you would meet only a small percentage who are passionate.

Surprisingly the Pereto's Principle of 80 : 20 is applicable here.

Let Us Recapitulate

- You could be passionate about certain activities which comes to you naturally. You might find yourself not liking certain activities at all. To get involved in activities which you don't relish, you can take efforts to mix other likeable activities, to create a likeable mix.

- Passion has been given to us by nature to keep us on track, and acts like an inner compass.

- Passion drives us to be ourselves.

- Passion is quite visible, and manifests in different colours.

- Many passionate people are close to being obsessive.

Your Personal Road Map

1. Name five people who are passionate about something. Name their likes.
2. How many could qualify for being obsessive out of these?
3. What is most striking about them pertaining to their personalities?
4. Name two people in each of the following professions who you think are passionate.
   - (a) Cricket
   - (b) Writers/authors
   - (c) Journalist
   - (d) Actors
   - (e) Entrepreneurs
   - (f) Scientist
   - (g) Senior corporate executives

   (h) Public figures

   (i) Political leaders

   (j) Film makers/directors

  (k) Sports person

   (l) Teachers

 (m) Doctors/therapists

  (n) Philanthropists

  (o) Architects/designers

  (p) Any other

5. Go to question 3. Do you have any such qualities? If yes, list them.

Passion, though a bad regulator, is a powerful spring.

– Ralph Waldo Emerson

2

What's Your Passion?
The Stuff that You are Made of

The most powerful weapon on earth is the human soul on fire.

- Field Marshal Ferdinand Foch

What Is Passion?

If Passion can change your life, bring happiness, get you success and satisfaction, and help you blossom to the fullest − then it is worth making an effort to find out what is your passion, because, it is the love of turning 'being' into action, and fuel the engine of creativity. We have only one life to live, and it would be worth living it at our own terms.

> Get excited and enthusiastic about your own dreams. This excitement is like a forest fire . . . you can smell it, taste it, and see it from a mile away.
>
> *− Anonymous*

Nature and your inner being signal about your likes and dislikes. Many a times we ignore these signals. In this chapter we are going to dig deeper, and make an effort to look for these signals, and amplify them for our own clarity. We are going to see how we can systematically look for these 'tell-tale marks'. You must have heard a lot of successful people saying that right from their childhood, they wanted to become actors, architects, or fashion designers. Many people say that they were fascinated by aircrafts, so they chose to become a pilot. Some people do identity their stimulant at an early age, and have their parents supporting them in letting them pursue it. They are also lucky to get into a profession which they loved right from their childhood. Its like marrying your childhood sweetheart.

Many people realise their potentials and their likes about a certain activity somewhere in mid career.

I know of great authors who started writing small articles for magazines as pastime, and for fun. As their work got recognised, they made further progress, and got into some serious writing – discovering their strong inclination during the journey itself. Another category of people get to know their strong preference after they retire from a very active, hectic, and a successful career. Those who choose to pursue it even after retirement, do extremely well, and make it into an even bigger career success – known as a second career.

Taking the example of Dr APJ Abdul Kalam, the former president of India, one would realise that triggers for your affinity can come from outside. From his childhood, he wanted to be a pilot in the air force and his father wanted him to join the Civil Services, until one day his school teacher taught them how a bird flies. He asked them to think from where does the bird get its power to fly, and Dr Kalam never stopped flying since that day. He didn't become a pilot, but he became a rocket scientist! Somehow the passion of flying, or making things fly got connected. I will discuss this later in the next chapter, wherein we will see how you can proliferate your passion.

Another important aspect to understand is the difference between love and infatuation. Sometimes you may get fascinated by something, which could be a small spike or a spark. It may not actually become a strong bonding. Linked to this fact is that, you must have the capacity, the talent, or the potential, to follow through what you really love to do. I may want to become a great musician, but I must have the basic talent. In fact, the capacity to follow is a very important requirement for success. One should be careful in understanding this connection, because the love of it, without requisite talent, can be a dangerous trap. We will discuss how to follow your strong likes in the next chapter.

Love is blind, but marriage is an eye opener.

— Anonymous

Even if you haven't been bowled over by any activity which can qualify to be called as your 'energy booster', there is always room to find some likes in the context of your present job. Some portions of your job could be very exciting, and some could be boring. Let us say that you have a job which involves working on a computer. You may not get excited typing letters or sending emails, but sometimes, when you get a task of making a presentation, blood starts racing through your head, and you are at your very best using all sorts of add-on software to create a power packed, highly flashy, and animated slide show! Your bosses love it, and your peers envy you looking at all this. Gradually, looking at this ability of yours, you may take on some additional courses in animation and graphics and get into that field, to finally find your passion.

Many a times you may not make a switch, but continue enjoying parts of your job that you love to do; in this case, you may volunteer to make slide shows all the time, and be happy that you enjoy your job because you get to make those exciting slide shows. It is worth testing the waters first and then making a change over. In fact, it is worth waiting before you make a change.

> You can't like all the things all the time, but you can like some of the things most of the times.

Let us say you are an engineer, well-settled in a job. You also like making oil paintings as a hobby. You have been at it for a few years, and over a period of time, made more than 25 paintings. One day your friend sees this collection which we assume is fairly impressive, and he suggests you to hold an exhibition. Obviously you have never thought of this, and you feel this to be an impossibility! Your friend also suggests a venue which is a vacant shop owned by his friend, and can be arranged at 1000 rupees for two days. You reluctantly agree, print 2000 hand bills for marketing and advertising at a small cost, and hold an exhibition. You sell eight paintings, and make a neat 25,000! You not only covered the cost of venue and advertising, you made a profit of more than 20,000 Rupees. Encouraged by this, you start taking your hobby seriously, and instead of wasting your holidays and weekends watching TV, you start painting with a new 'Josh'. In about a couple of years, you make about 40 paintings. You also act upon the feedback from the last exhibition, realising that people love your roses more than your horses and landscapes. So, you deliberately concentrate more on roses this time.

Having done all this, you check out the rates for booking a good art gallery, and you realise that it would cost you less than your profits earned from your last venture. You go ahead and book the venue, give a small advertisement in the papers, and exhibit your paintings for the second time at a much larger scale. You not only sell a good number of paintings – at a much better price than earlier, but also manage to get a few interviews in the daily newspapers (with a photograph of course)! You have arrived. Over a couple of years, you feel that you are making more money than your regular job – its time to change. You found your passion, and in it, your new profession.

Each individual creature on this beautiful planet is created by God to fulfil a particular role.

– Dr APJ Abdul Kalam

At campus placement, at business schools, I often hear young boys and girls saying that they are looking out for a particular job profile. Although it is good to look for jobs where the job content matches your abilities, but it should not be taken too seriously at this stage of life, at least not as the only major criterion for accepting a job offer. A simple reason for this is, that it is too early at that stage to know what you really like and what you don't, and what you are capable of and what you are not.

One should take up his/her first job which essentially matches his/her qualification and profile. I feel one should experiment for a while thereafter, to discover their best fit. In any case, if you want to learn and find what you like, you must stay hungry and stay foolish. Hunger is a desire to learn, and by acting foolishly, you are able to experiment without getting too worried about whether you are right or wrong.

This book is not about making a career switch, but about making your career more enjoyable, and making a change when the time is right. I am also not trying to give a straight jacket formula like a 'one size fits all solution'; you have to make efforts to find what you like.

Another angle to be considered is our 'inherited potential'. We inherit a lot from our parents. In fact, Mandel's Law goes on to say that we could inherit certain diseases, traits, characteristics, or even talents from our ancestors, going back seven generations. Mandel was an Austrian monk, who researched in the area of genetics in the nineteenth century. Even Darwin was aware that hidden traits could emerge after several generations. Our vedic literature '*shastras*' also reveal that certain traits or characteristics of an individual are hereditary, and have their influence upto seven generations. Our thoughts, preferences, actions, and wishes, therefore go back to our ancestral past. Therefore, you see music running in families. The laws of nature being so complex, it is possible that out of four sons of a great musician, only one blossoms as a good artist. Therefore, you could get certain clues about your inherited potential by looking closely at your own family, and maybe digging a little deeper into the history of your roots. From the practical viewpoint, your father or grandfather may not have possessed what you have, because your great grandfather did! So don't worry if your real brothers and sisters are not good at mathematics and logical reasoning; but you could very well be. Many a times it could well become your inherited capital; your parents wouldn't have left much real estate, gold, and money for you, but you may have inherited some very good traits and talents, which could well compensate.

We as human beings are capable of discovering new and better ways to do everything, and even doing more with less. We have always been fighting droughts, floods and jungle fires, which created scarcity. This hard–wired 'dog eats dog' culture is within us, and we always want to win against the odds. Therefore, the concept of 'I win you lose', because 'in – a – fight – both – can't – win' went deep down into us. Survival is tough, so our orientations have always been towards survival and money–making activities, rather than pursuing passion. That is why parents (who inherit this trait from their parents) always ask children to focus on jobs and job-oriented learning.

Every human being is designed and fabricated to be passionate. It is like a flame in our hearts or a torch in our heads which shows us the direction and gives us the energy to move ahead in that direction. This flame in the heart remains alive through our memories and our experiences, good or bad. But if it is not fuelled or refuelled, it slowly dies down. This tiny flame, if ignored, is analogous to forgetting refuelling your car. The best part is that, memories never die – they can always be rekindled.

We do not see things as they are; we see things as we are.

– The Talmind

Your Own Profile

To find what you love to do (If someone tells you), you must make an effort to look at your basic characteristics. This would help in moving on to the next step. Let us take one step at a time. These will also indicate your negatives in terms of convictions, values, and your expressions. In a way, you will know why you are as you are today. Relate yourself to these parameters, and it will be easier for you to come closer to what you love.

• Your Memories

I mentioned earlier that the flame of your heart is preserved in your memory. Your negative and positive experiences are also preserved in the form of memory. You relate and interpret your present world with your experiences through your memory. I have a friend who, out of our group of friends, never picked up smoking, whereas we all smoked regularly. The reason was that, his father was a heavy smoker and used to ask him to go and buy cigarettes for him at odd hours, sometimes in scorching heat or heavy rain, when he was a small child; and he hated it. So much so that he started hating cigarettes and in his subconscious mind decided never to touch a cigarette! Anyway good for him.

Similarly, if you saw your mother playing a sitar during your childhood, you may at some point of time try playing some musical instrument. If you were in your teens in the seventies, and you listen to a song of that era, you are suddenly propelled back into those days. All the memories of those days come rushing back. Memory is a powerful tool to connect with your passion and your likes.

• **Your Values**

In simple words, values are important for you. Is it health, money, family life, freedom, power, and achievement you want in life? For some people, freedom and autonomy at work may be the most important parameter. In fact, whatever you value, you tend to spend maximum effort in that area if you like being healthy then it is the gym, the tennis court that you frequent more than the pubs. If it is money, you would be reading financial reports and magazines. If it is music, then you would be listening to your favourite music and might have pictures of great singers pasted on the walls of your room.

Best things in life are not things.

– Art Buchwald

Few values or human valuables are listed as under:

Being the best	Pride	Learning	Adventure	Simplicity
Determination	Success	Health	Competition	Discipline
Stability	Achievement	Power	Happiness	Equality
Fun	Warmth	Creativity	Wealth	Respect

Once you have listed your valuables, then it is time to prioritise them. I am using the word valuables because the word 'value' goes more into an idealistic mode, as if on a high pedestal.

I want you to write what gives you a thrill, a kick, a high. Let it be power, money, fame, or whatever. I have a friend whose son did his computer engineering from IIT, Delhi. Obviously, a bright guy, he joined a software company in Bangalore, the IT capital of India. On one occasion, while he was in his office, there was some riot-like situation in the city. This was flashed on the radio and TV. Suddenly, he saw a police inspector moving into the area and he (by authority of his uniform) made all the shops and offices close down within minutes. This young boy got so impressed by this, that he made a mental note that if there is power, then it is with the police. He sat for the Civil Services exam, made it to the Indian Administrative Services, but, opted for the Indian Police Service (IPS)! Values are, to some extent, your guides to your likes and your passion.

If you are clear about what your values are, or what you really value, it will become easier for you to set your goals in alignment with your likes. You can become more realistic than being idealistic. For example, if fame and money are your values and acting is your Passion then it is good to get into films rather than become a stage actor, because stage acting can fulfil the desire of acting but will not let you get fame and money. That can only be met through films. If writing is what you like only fiction can get you fame and not a book on rocket science as everybody reads fiction and very few read rocket science. So you got to align your values with your talent and inspiration.

Values also give you a guiding awareness for making appropriate changes in your behaviour, so that you act and behave according to them. It also lets you assess whether your values match with your present profession, as well as your present organisation and bosses that you work for.

Therefore, it is very important to make a list of your values and priorities. They then become the rules of thumb for moving into your energy zone.

Your Values match with $\longrightarrow$ Passion

$\longrightarrow$ Behaviour

$\longrightarrow$

$\longrightarrow$ Present Profession

$\longrightarrow$ Organisation

• Your Convictions

Convictions are actually straight pointers to your passion, and also give you the wings to follow your likes, and discard your dislikes. This also gives you faith in yourself. Unfortunately, negative convictions can become stumbling blocks.

> One of the secrets of life is to make stepping stones out of stumbling blocks.
>
> *– Jack Penn*

If you are convinced that you can crack an exam, then you can. Convictions must get connected with dreams. For example, you see a lot of ramp shows, fashion competitions and international beauty pageants; and you want to be there. The 'distance' between being there and not being there is now a question of conviction. If you feel you can do it, then you can, and then you can be there. Therefore, some of your convictions could be 'hard work always pays' or 'reading is the best way to go ahead', or 'honesty is the best policy'.

• Your Medium of Expression

Human beings widely differ from other species, and that difference is in our expression, medium of communication, or language. We can think by using this medium, and we can imagine using the power of expression. Animals can't think as to what they will be doing on a weekend! You must develop the power of expression in the area that you value. If you want to excel in management, then you must learn the right terminologies and jargons. If you want to be in human resource consultancy, then you must develop that vocabulary. With the medium of expression, we can not only convince ourselves, but can also convince others.

Earlier, the officers of the British Armed Forces were made to believe that the armed forces were meant to serve the country and valour, and not to make money. During the British Raj, this was trickled down to the Indian Armed Forces. It got so hard–wired into the Indian officer class that earning money, was something like a taboo. Quite a foggy idea and ideal though. So much so that the first generation Indian officers after the British left were so enamoured with this idea (Planted in their heads by British expression) that they never saved even for their retirement and often found themselves without money.

• Your Personal Decisions

Someone who decides from his teens that he wants to make a lot of money in life, will have a very different way of life and thinking, than someone who doesn't. I know of a friend who joined the government service, but within a few years, decided that he would quit the service and open a computer consultancy firm. He directed his efforts and (he liked handling computer hardware and software) attended various courses to upgrade his skills. Precisely at the right time, he quit the service, and started his company. His present status was the reflection of a decision taken much earlier in life. He identified his value (money, autonomy) and took a decision.

• Your Attitude

In simple words, attitude is your perception, viewpoint, and your opinion about anything. This is based on your experiences, your background your values, and what you believe in. If, for example, courage and courage of conviction is what you value, then you have an attitude which is conducive to follow your heart.

Remember a little while ago, we discussed how an engineer became a professional painter? He must have had courage to take the first step of holding his first exhibition, and then the courage to work hard, listen to others, take feedback, and go professional. Therefore, assessing your attitude is very important, so that you can remove those negative vibes out of your attitude, which would help you in following and pursuing your chosen path.

Make an effort to analyse yourself against these parameters. Make a very broad attempt, and don't get into many details. Yet, you will be able to get that gut feeling about yourself, as to what stuff you are made of. Having done that, you now have to listen to your heart, and say, 'These are a few of my favourite things'.

Listening to Your Heart: Your Likes and Dislikes

The next logical step would be to answer some very simple questions about your preferences, and draw inferences out of the answers that you get. As you look at your likes and dislikes, a pattern would emerge which will be a strong indicator of your passions.

• What is the Activity that you are Prepared to do Free of Cost?

As I mentioned earlier, we are programmed for survival. Most of our activities are directed towards money-making, and are called productive goals. We all feel very insecure about our present as well as our future, as far as finances are concerned. More so, in developing nations like India, where there is no social security or old age pension, one tends to be focused on savings for the future. In this scenario if you want to follow your passion, then you must ask yourself as to what is the activity that you love to do, and you can do repeatedly without being paid for it. Before you answer this question, I would like to mention that whatever you love to do, will be eventually paid for, but you must be ready to do it for free.

Let us put this question differently. What if all your needs are taken care of, and you have nothing to worry about? What will be the activity you would love to do then? Someone may say 'Oh if

I had all the money in the world, I would go into the mountains and camp there, and go for long treks, rappling, and skiing'. I know a friend who served in the army for quite a number of years, and was fond of mountain adventure. He had been a trained mountaineer and a seasoned sportsman. After he quit the army, he started taking people for adventure sports, and set up a roaring business. He loved being in the mountains, and got satisfaction as well as money for it. Think of all the activities for which you would say 'Oh I wish I had the time and freedom to do that'. Now that is an indicator of what actually your heart wants.

• What do you Love to do? and are you Prepared to take a Risk for it?

You must make a list of activities that you love to do, even if there is a risk involved. Adolf Hitler used to love getting into political discussions, and he wanted to become an architect! After the defeat of Germany in the World War 1, there used to be a lot of political debates across German towns. He used to jump into the fray with his drawing board, and a Tee Square in his hands, and speak his heart out. He took the risk of speaking his mind and heart out, when things were not in a good shape in Germany. So go ahead, and list all that you love, and for which you can risk your neck out. It could be going out with your friends, watching movies, writing articles on subjects which could be controversial, getting into intellectual argument, and even going on a tangent while the discussions are on. Do you know that Bhagwan Rajneesh, popularly known, as 'Osho' used to argue a lot. He always had an answer for anything that was asked from him as a child. He spoke what he thought was right, and was open to criticism. He kept this habit alive, and convinced millions of his followers later about his philosophy of life. He could have been a great lawyer with these capabilities, or even a successful political leader! The price for what you love doing could be criticism, people calling you crazy, losing a job, losing a friend, and even loss of some money. So be prepared to identify your love, and be prepared for a little risk.

• Do you get Angry about Something?

I love dogs, and I hate anybody ill-treating an animal, especially a dog, and I have picked up a fight on a couple of occasions for this. I get very upset and angry when someone ill-treats helpless animals. This could well give me a clue to my strong likes. I never thought of it before, but as I write, I feel I can open a successful kennel.

Mahatma Gandhi was thrown out of the train in South Africa. He got angry against injustice. It became a resolve, a movement, and then liberation of a country. So watch what you get angry about. You can get a valuable clue to what you want to do. Connect it with your values discussed earlier, and you may get a hidden link. If Mahatma Gandhi was to be asked what his values were, I am sure freedom and justice would be his top priority. Coupled with what he got angry about it got him committed passionately for a freedom fight.

• Why do I Love my Job?

Many of us would say, 'I generally don't love my job, but I like only a part of it, and if my boss asks me to do just that part only, then I would love to do it all the time'. Now this could provide a valuable clue to your likes. For example, working as a system integrator, you are supposed to perform a number of functions like pilot project and review, project definition, project management and presales, and technical support. It is quite likely that you love the presales part, involving discussions and presentations at a macro level. If this is what you love in your job, then maybe you are more cut-out for marketing than technology. This would also tell you what comes most naturally to you.

• What came Easily to you in your Earlier Jobs?

We switch jobs, and each of this we add to our CV as work experience. One of the best things to learn from those experiences is to find out what your likes are, and what parts of the job you enjoyed more. As managers, most of us have to perform a large number of job functions. Each of these is an opportunity to learn what we love to do. You should also go back to your childhood and see which small jobs gave you a thrill.

• What Puts You Off at Work?

No work environment can ever be perfect, and you always have some pinpricks which trouble you at work. You can always draw some lessons from these negatives. You can understand what is suppressing your enthusiasm, and take corrective actions. You can also make an effort to get these negatives out of your organisation. For example, a common problem which many of us face at work is the lack of appreciation and bosses taking you for granted. If this puts you off, then you know that to work with people who are appreciative of your efforts, would enhance your performance, and get your enthusiasm back.

Sometimes people are caught between their own values and values of their bosses, or that of the organisation. When you examine your own values a little more closely under these circumstances, you tend to get some ideas about your passion, because ideals, values, and passion are closely linked. Sometimes lack of freedom or autonomy at work, because of organisational culture, hierarchy, or power, can also stunt your enthusiasm and curb your initiative. So you know your major strengths and creativity can only blossom when you are given a freehand. In my previous organisation, for example, I always felt that claustrophobic feeling of being choked, because everything worked too procedurally for my liking. I wanted encouragement and freedom, and that came in my way to give my best.

Organisation for which I worked for earlier, must have lost some of my good ideas, but at the end of the day, I, as an individual, may have been the bigger loser. If you are in such a situation, it is time to change your job, and the faster you do, the better it is for you. Therefore, I would like to work with people who give me a freehand, provide encouragement, and appreciate my work. More importantly, I learnt a lesson that these things are harmful for the organisation, as well as your subordinates. Therefore, as the head of an organisation, I give full freedom to my subordinates to take initiatives, and I always make it a point to appreciate them whenever it is required.

If we resist our passion, it is more through our weakness than our strength.

– Anonymous

Your most Whacky Expectation

Since you have gone through your profile and also looked at your likes and dislikes, it's time to go in for the kill, and against this backdrop, make a wish list – the wackier, the better. You assume that if everything under the sun was possible to achieve, then what would you like to do or achieve in the following domains? Remember there are no limits, it is limited only by your imagination.

- Personal
- Family and home
- Money and finances
- Your career or job
- Social cause

Write down two achievements in each of the areas mentioned earlier.

Mind Blockers

By now you know your own personality, perceptions, your likes, and your goals and expectations. At this point of time, you should be able to make a list of the areas that prevent you from achieving and fulfilling your expectations. We have been programmed to think in a particular way, and many a times say to ourselves, 'How the hell can I do this' or 'I think it's too late in the day to do all that', or 'I don't think I have the capability to do that'. These are all mind blockers. I want you to stretch your imagination, and imagine yourself doing what you want to do.

A mind that is stretched to a new idea, never returns to its original dimension.

– *Oliver Wendell Holmes*

Flirting and Experimenting

Many if not all cases of love affairs begin with a bit of flirting. Instead of giving it a negative connotation, I would view it as 'the explore and experiment' phase of love. If love before marriage is not a taboo, then flirting before love may be taken as a step prior to falling in love.

I talked briefly about attitude earlier. Tonnes of material is available on attitude, yet most of us don't have the right one. According to me, the most important aspect about attitude which could help in finding your passion is the attitude of experimenting. This could be an attitude in almost everything that you do. Attitude, remember, is a very broad behavioural stance of individuals. When you say he has a negative attitude, then the guy will be negative about almost everything on the earth. An enthusiastic attitude means that the fellow will be generally enthusiastic about almost everything. Let me explain what is an experimental attitude. When you go out for lunch to an Udipi restaurant, do you usually order masala dosa with sambhar? Now have you tried masala dosa with rasam? Let me tell you it tastes great. 'No way, I like it only with sambhar and I have been having it at this restaurant for the last 20 years!' You protest and justify. You are not even prepared to experiment once.

Going to Baskin Robbins, I always order two scoops of coffee chocolate chip. Why can't I have one scoop of coffee chocolate chip, and another one of black current? Next time, try something different – there are dozens of flavours, remember. Going for Chinese, I have always ordered Chinese hot and sour chicken soup or sweet corn chicken soup! Why not try something different? This is lack of experimental attitude. Go for a picnic in rains, try out different clothes, listen not only to pop, but also to jazz; see comedy, suspense, as well as art films. Read different types of books on different subjects, and by different authors. The world is huge, and there is lot to savour and taste. So go for it. Experiment.

Steps to Find out Your Passion

By now, you have gone wackier, wiser, and ready to explore. So it's time to flirt and take systematic steps to get to the bottom of it. Passion is a single, yet powerful emotional experience, which is internal and personal.

We got to disconnect ourselves with the hectic day-to-day life that we lead, and that is the time you can connect your head to your heart, and more importantly, listen to what your heart has to tell you. Let us look at basic actions that you can take to find your true love.

• Become Sensitive and get Connected to Yourself

Now this sounds very cliché – doesn't it. But it is true. In simple terms, you need a bit of time, some leisure time to fool around, and that's where you strike the chord. You know most of my new ideas come to me in the restroom, or while having a bath. I don't know if it is the fragrance of the soap, peace of mind, or something else. Recent research work indicates that your subconscious database hugely outweighs the conscious one, on an order exceeding a million to one! This database is the source of your hidden natural genius. This is the wonder of a relaxed mind. So take some free time – doing nothing – say a walk, a jog, sitting idle for some time during the day, maybe just stargazing at night.

In fact, this confirms the fact that your gut, the heart, and the mind, get connected when you are doing nothing worthwhile, and bathing is one such activity. Today, you don't have time to go and lie down on grass and do some bird-watching in the day or stargazing at night. Actually, such activities, or similar ones when your mind is totally free, let you understand your innermost feelings. Therefore, take a break once in a while, and pay close attention to what excites you, inspires you, and even annoys you. Books, television shows, and simple conversation with friends, will give you some clues of what you possibly want from life.

Don't look for your heart's response too seriously; you can't find it that way. Take it easy, be in flow, experiment, and explore, and most importantly, get some time free for yourself, to get what you want.

You continue meeting people, and the right person would strike the chord one day.

• Explore your Mind and your Gut

Ask yourself some simple questions, and try to answer them candidly.

(a) What would you like to do if you knew that you would always succeed?

For example, if you are confident that if you go for a television audition, you are sure to get selected. Then write down this fact somewhere, because this is your talent, your confidence, and that's what you are good at.

(b) What do you like about yourself?

Ok, I have my voice and that would be Amitabh Bachchan's answer. Someone may say, I like my beautiful face, or I love the way I do up the interiors of my home. All these are strong pointers to passions and professions. Ladies who have had the knack of doing up their homes and pushed themselves a little, have become very successful interior designers.

(c) What do you dream about when you are doing nothing, or having a bath?

This is called day dreaming and it is good to fantasise, crave, and think of all that you want to do.

(d) To get clues, go back into history.

What did I love when I was in school? What was that one thing in college on which I was willing to spend most of my time? I loved watching cricket and talked about all day long. I could discuss every player and dissect every shot. Also, if you have a good voice and the right diction, you can be a good commentator!

(e) Can you describe yourself in one word or in one sentence?

Some would say, 'I can explain a point very well, oh yes! I am a born teacher'. 'I can argue my way out of every situation, I am a born lawyer, or even a politician'. I don't have statistics to prove, but most politicians have been lawyers. Alternatively, lawyers make good politicians – you bet.

(f) What would you love to do if money was not a consideration?

This will give you an idea of what you love to do right from the bottom of your heart. If I get to play with a good beat group, let me assure you, I can play drums for the whole night for free!

(g) What are those hidden desires which you are afraid of sharing with others?

This happens when we feel 'what would others feel about this?' or 'I think people will laugh at me'. You want to become an actor and you think your friends will say, 'Hey, you and acting, are you nuts?' That is why I said earlier; be prepared to fool around, and be prepared to face the world, face the world and face failure, and you will succeed. If you see Hrithik Roshan, he took a big risk by playing a mentally challenged boy in *Koi Mil Gaya*, it was an experiment which required courage and confidence. As an actor, he was doing very well, but he was prepared to experiment.

(h) Can I contribute something to the people or the world?

This sounds very idealistic, but let me put it this way, that if you can make people laugh, you have done something positive for the people, and you can get into comedy. Let me tell you that most of the comedians have a great sense of humour from their childhood, and they have this skill which they develop into a successful profession. They make the world laugh, and that's how they contribute to the world. I want to become a doctor, and that's how I want to contribute. Ok, I want to become a marriage counsellor or a motivator, and that is how I would contribute. It is also a matter of perception.

• Finding a Career which would Excite You

There are various reasons for people to be happy or unhappy with their jobs. But, whichever profession you have chosen, there are always a few things or some portions of the job you like very much, and some you don't. Therefore, each one of us gets some sense of satisfaction, and a sense of achievement at workplace. Many a times, sense of accomplishment comes from a personal, deeper meaning, when you are involved with an important cause or a larger reason than money.

Therefore, each one of us has certain 'inner drivers', which give us the necessary fuel to go along and do our jobs well. In the most blunt form, it could be the smell of cordite that gives a high to a sharp shooter, or the smell of rubber from screeching tyres on a Formula 1 racing track that makes a world champion. People who hate the smell of anesthesia and develop cold feet going to the operation theatre, shouldn't try to become surgeons. So now, let us look at some professions which provide an opportunity to fulfil our desires or our drivers.

> Trouble with gardening is that, it does not remain an avocation, it becomes an obsession.
>
> — *Phyllis M C Ginley*

Drive Cluster	Leads to	Profession Cluster
1. Science/Maths Logical Reasons		Engineers, staticians, programmers, doctors, chartered accountants, scientists.
2. Money and Material		Doctors, film stars, stock brokers, high flying executives, merchant navy officers, politicians, lawyers.
3. Patriotism		Armed forces, police, paramilitary.
4. Adrenaline/ Adventure/ Danger		Adventure sports, formula racing, fighter pilots, bodyguards, bouncers, hit men, fishing in high seas, coastguards, search and rescue, firefighters, miners.
5. Glamour		Fashion designers, models, actors, high, profile writers/authors, photographers, TV anchors, DJs, astronauts.
6. Research/ Investigative		Detectives, research scientists, journalists, forensic scientists, writers/ authors, stasticians.
7. Loving Some Specific Things		Pet groomers, pilots, horticulturists, art importers.

8.	Expression, Language and Intellect	Lawyers, writers, playwriters, copywriter, talk show anchors, RJs, sports announcers, commentators, magazine editors.
9.	Environment	Farmers, mountaineers, field biologists, merchant navy officers.
10.	Performance	Politicians, trainers, motivational speakers, trial lawyers, code breakers, actors.
11.	Creativity	Musicians, actors, painters, sculptors, photographers, interior designers, writers, graphic designers, fashion designers, screenwriters, winemakers, animators, flashy car designers.
12.	People and Masses	Teachers, actors, mediators, politicians, sales and marketing people.
13.	Status and Prestige/Power	Executives, heads of business schools, politicians, civil servants, doctors.
14.	Cause and Personal Satisfaction	Coaches and counsellors, teachers, social workers, healthcare professionals, armed forces, police, doctors, social workers.

I have listed more than a dozen clusters of drivers and the professions they lead to. You would notice that it is a many-to-many relation, which means, one driver can lead to many professions, and conversely, one profession is driven by many drivers. Therefore, when you are excited about a career, it is not a single driver, but a number of them which make you choose a profession. For example, if you look at acting as a profession, it is driven by creativity, performance, glamour, adrenaline, people, and money. Politicians are driven by performance, status, prestige and power. Unfortunately, politicians across the world are not driven by patriotism! And that is a fact. Most of the times they are driven more by money than anything else. There is, therefore, no 'perfect fit' solution. As long as the basic requirements of your drivers are met, you are moving in line with your passion.

Also, please don't look into the other guy's plate, when you have found yours. If as a mountaineer, your drive for a good environment and adrenaline has been met, then don't look for power, prestige, and intellect in mountaineering.

By now, you have done enough—you have looked at passions, your personal profile, likes and dislikes, most whacky expectations, mind blockers, and the need to experiment. I have listed a number of drivers which motivate us, and I have also given the related cluster of professions. The list is not exhaustive, but definitely indicative. Now let us move forward to make our 'passion profile' using these drivers.

Writing your Passion Profile

For this, you must discard external factors like peer comparison or personal family commitments, financial constraints, etc. We bust-up our feelings, so that we can be accepted in the context of what others say. How can you live your life on the preferences and judgements made by others? Be a child and say what you want to say and write what you want to write. Out of the 14 drivers that I have listed, pick up seven that you feel can motivate you. Then give priorities to them from the first to seventh. Don't analyse, but use the brainstorming techniques and your basic instincts. With this first step, you have knocked off seven drivers already. Now have a re-look at these seven drivers that you have shortlisted. Now make it shorter. Knock it down to three, or maximum five.

It could well be under one for us. I get driven by these five clusters in the order of priority.

1. Prestige and power

2. People and masses

3. Performance

4. Glamour

5. Creativity

Now try to figure out what professions your drivers lead to. Also, you must keep at the back of your mind, what are you good at. Then, try to match your drivers with your capabilities to look for the right fit. If you become a motivational speaker, a write, and a teacher par excellence – you would be able to get all of them. Think of Deepak Chopra or Stephen Covey. If you ask any of them about their drivers, I am sure four out of the five drivers listed above would be true for each one of them! They have prestige, they perform as speakers, they meet people, they have glamour or style, and they have used creativity to reach there! Are you getting the point? And mind you, money is a BONUS for both of them.

Expanding your Horizon

You can experiment only if you have something to experiment with. To give yourself more opportunities, you must make conscious efforts to get more opportunities. There are a number of innovative ways, but I feel the following would be of great help.

• Meeting People from Different Professions

This is a simple way of opening the floodgates. Unfortunately, I have seen that we are very comfortable within our own zones.

When a few air force officers get together then within five minutes of their meeting they will start discussing only flying and their old incidences. If software professionals meet they can only discuss coding problems even while enjoying a drink together. When army officers meet they discuss their old stories of yesteryears. Give me a break – I need to know about other activities and things that people do. For that it is very essential to meet people from other professions and understand what they do. These can give wonderful clues and in any case you start thinking out of the box because you have literally moved out of the box!

• Attending Seminars, Meets, and Workshops

Here again, you are trying to take inputs from various experts on different domains. You get to know a lot about what is going on outside your activity zone. Thereafter, as a software engineer, if you get a chance to attend a seminar on motivation, don't miss the opportunity. Many a times we focus only on the vertical horizon and don't move horizontally – that's why we can't expand our horizons! Horizons are horizontal!

• Reading Biographies

I will discuss role models in the next chapter. But reading biographies of people from different domains (now that is important) is likely to give you ideas about other professions and drivers. Don't read only about world leaders like John F. Kennedy, Winston Churchill, and Hitler. Expand your horizon by reading about great scientists, entrepreneurs, educationists, soldiers, mountaineers, etc. Again, the idea is to move horizontally.

Let us Recapitulate

• Passion propels performance, and therefore, it is worth looking for your passion.

- You can discover Passion at any age and stage of life.

- It is important to understand the difference between deep love and infatuation, because a casual infatuation can lead you to a dangerous trap.

- You can always find some portions of your job that excite you, and thereby, you can make your job more meaningful.

- If you want to make a change, then it is worthwhile to test the waters before you take the plunge.

- You must also look at the inherited potential which has been passed on to you by your parents in the form of talent, dedication, etc.

- Your own profile is the first step to looking at yourself. Your values, memories, convictions, expressions, attitude, and decisions make your profile.

- Listen to your heart and make a list of your likes and dislikes.

- Right down your most outrageous expectations in life.

- Be prepared to experiment.

- Look at different career options and the drivers which attract people to different jobs. This would help you in identifying what career moves you should make.

- Write down your essence, the gut or the core of your passion. Shortlist your options, and then narrow them down to three or five at the most. Now try to match these with professions that could satisfy your passion profile.

- Expand your horizon by meeting people from different professions, attending seminars and discussions, and reading biographies of great people from different professions.

Table (a): Skills – cluster of skills required for the listed professions

Skills	Teachers	Soldiers	Politicians	Civil Servants	Doctors	Journalists	TV Anchors	Lawyers	Sports-men	Graphic Designers
Must have	Communications skills, knowledge									
Should have	Going into details, being articulate									
Could have	Empathy, good Personality									

Table (B): Drivers - Cluster of Drivers Required for the Listed Professions

Drivers	Teachers	Soldiers	Politicians	Civil Servants	Doctors	Journalists	TV Anchors	Lawyers	Sports-men	Graphic Designers
Must have	Art of explaining a point									
Should have	Public speaking people									
Could have	A less pressured job, research orientation									

YOUR PERSONAL ROAD MAP

1. Attempt this simple exercise where you should write the skills required for 10 professions that are listed under. Skills are clusters of must haves, should haves, and could haves. Think hard and you can identify a good number of them. The answers for teaching as a profession are given in the exercise. This would give you an idea how to fill up rest of the Table (A). Thereafter, fill up the drivers in the same way for Table (B).

2. To get an idea how passionate you are in general and how much potential do you have to raise your passion levels, rate yourself on the scale of 1 to 7 given as under:

	Are You?	No								Yes
1.	Are you enthusiastic?	No	1	2	3	4	5	6	7	Yes
2.	Do you think out of the box?	No	1	2	3	4	5	6	7	Yes
3.	Do you think you are an achiever?	No	1	2	3	4	5	6	7	Yes
4.	Are you risk taking?	No	1	2	3	4	5	6	7	Yes
5.	Are you a dreamer?	No	1	2	3	4	5	6	7	Yes
6.	Do you get involved in most activities?	No	1	2	3	4	5	6	7	Yes
7.	Do you think big?	No	1	2	3	4	5	6	7	Yes
8.	Do you like challenges?	No	1	2	3	4	5	6	7	Yes
9.	Are you persistant?	No	1	2	3	4	5	6	7	Yes
10.	Are you generally interested in a lot of things?	No	1	2	3	4	5	6	7	Yes
11.	Are you obsessive?	No	1	2	3	4	5	6	7	Yes
12.	Are you energetic?	No	1	2	3	4	5	6	7	Yes

13.	Are you inquisitive?	No	1	2	3	4	5	6	7	Yes
14.	Are you focused?	No	1	2	3	4	5	6	7	Yes
15.	Are you excited about new things?	No	1	2	3	4	5	6	7	Yes
16.	Are you prepared to experiment in general?	No	1	2	3	4	5	6	7	Yes
17.	Are you innovative?	No	1	2	3	4	5	6	7	Yes
18.	Are you creative?	No	1	2	3	4	5	6	7	Yes
19.	Are you prepared to put behind status and money for what you love doing?	No	1	2	3	4	5	6	7	Yes
20.	Do you compete with yourself?	No	1	2	3	4	5	6	7	Yes
21.	Do others think you are full of life?	No	1	2	3	4	5	6	7	Yes
22.	Do you think there is still a child in you?	No	1	2	3	4	5	6	7	Yes
23.	Are you prepared to try something new and make a fool of yourself?	No	1	2	3	4	5	6	7	Yes
24.	Are you prepared to break rules and do something unusual?	No	1	2	3	4	5	6	7	Yes

If you answer these honestly, and mark it realistically, you will get a fair idea about your passionate nature, and your capability to follow your heart. Note down the areas where you scored less than 4, and try to make a change in all those qualities.

Disclaimer: The above test is not statistically validated and checked for reliability.

3. Write down 10 values of yours (or valuables, as described in the chapter).

   (a)   (f)

   (b)   (g)

   (c)   (h)

    (d)   (i)

    (e)   (j)

Now prioritise them and then shortlist only five of these.

    (a)

    (b)

    (c)

    (d)

    (e)

4. List five major convictions of yours. These are your beliefs at a deeper level. These could be your personal slogans or statements, or even resolves.

    (a)

    (b)

    (c)

    (d)

    (e)

5. List three most memorable events of yours.

    (a)

    (b)

    (c)

Now try to analyse why these were the most memorable events. Also make an effort to relate these good feelings with your likes and passion. Going into the past could help you identify your passion.

You can't sweep other people off their feet, if you can't be swept off your own.

– Clarence Day

3

Implementing Passion to Achieve Goals

Walk the Talk

Jesus gave me the message, Gandhi gave me the method.

— Martin Luther King Jr.

By now you must be having a good idea about your profile and your likes and dislikes. It must also be clear to you as to what tickles you at the core, and you would have made a list of professions or occupations which suit your temperament, what you love, and which could be in line with your basic drivers. Let me tell you, you are more than half way through, as far as making a success out of yourself is concerned. Before we move forward, let us look at some basic facts.

Some Facts

More than 50 per cent of close to a million small businesses, which in the US in 1998, were based on hobbies or personal interest of the people. People in all these cases made a living out of what they really loved. Other than business, I would say that all those who chose sports, fine arts, and occupations motivated by creativity, are also into it because of passion. People who are into the so-called 'productive money–making professions' are successful, because they add a generous dash of love to their work. If you look at the lives of the Beatles, Elvis Presley, A R Rahman, Albert Einstein, Narayana Murthy, Adolf Hitler and great scientists or doctors, you would find that all of them loved what they chose to do. There are hundreds of people in each profession, then why are only a few successful? These few are the ones who get involved in their work because they like their work.

> In all great leaders there is a purpose and intensity which is unmistakable.
>
> *– Ron Hubbard*

Are you professional about your business, or passionate about it? The difference is the key. Out of two Japanese car manufacturing companies, one was perpetually concentrating on profitability and long-term business goals, and the other company focussed on, and was a leader in product performance. The company which focussed on producing better cars was obviously more passionate about its business. Therefore, it was no surprise that the second company attracted more people to work for it. In addition, the attrition rate (employees leaving the company) was much smaller for the company which was proud of its product, rather than profitability. I would like to mention here that, instead of changing your hobby into work, you can always make your work a hobby. It is just the way you look at it. I will discuss about involvement a little later.

Thumb Rules to Live Your Passion

• Be Prepared to Notch Down

When we see the whole world around us organised to behave in a particular way, it is but natural that our thinking will get influenced accordingly. Over a period of time, we have learnt that success is measured in terms of the wealth and things that we possess. These are the trappings of success; big house, a couple of cars, designation on your visiting card, bank balance, etc. We do manage to collect all this in some measure or the other. If you want to follow what you love, then you must be prepared to sacrifice some of these, and this is the most difficult part of the process. In case of those who are married, it is important that both, husband and wife, should take joint decisions on matters of consideration. Because, if a decision is taken in isolation, then it can cause problems in the relationship.

If you have been watching the television shows, then you might recall Debojit from Assam, who became the 'Voice of India' in a singing competition. His wife supported all his actions. In fact, she had taken the entire load of running the home so that her husband could concentrate on his singing. In fact, half the battle is won if your family supports your choice of profession.

• Simplify your Life

There is an old saying, 'Simple living and high thinking'. I feel this would come handy now.

> It has never been about money for me. Money is just a convenient way of keeping score.
>
> – *Donald Trump*

We, in fact, spend our entire life and efforts just to keep the score. Yes, keeping the score. Therefore, we don't enjoy playing the match. While pondering over your values in the last chapter, if simplicity and simple living was high on your value chain, then be rest assured, it will be very easy to follow what you love to do. Conversely, this is the biggest stumbling block for people while deciding to go in for their passion. Many films show that a rich girl falls in love with a poor boy and is determined to marry him against the wishes of her parents. The girl's prime argument is that, she would be able to live with him even in a small house, and with the least amount of money. Cinema is a reflection of our real lives. Similarly, if you can be prepared to simplify and manage with in less money then it will be easy to follow your dream.

• Be Flexible

Flexibility in general is a great virtue and an asset. Now this is important. Following your passion blindly may not be a wise thing. In the context of a dream and making it work, you must be prepared to be flexible. If you are into music, and people want jazz, don't insist on playing rock. This would be suicidal. In fact, many a times when you see talented people fail while following their passion, it is because of their 'rigidity', or lack of flexibility. If people appreciate horses that you paint, then don't insist on making portraits – align your likes with the market requirements. Remember you have to eventually make a living out of it. Good actors polish themselves with time, as they sense what the audience wants, and then act according to what is in demand.

Marilyn Johnson Kondwani today owns a cosmetic company, and writes about the subject on various platforms. Her inspiration came from those ravishing advertisements of Revlon, where she saw those beautiful faces of women splashed across the magazines. She, being a coloured women, had an obvious disadvantage. But she was so inspired by the glamour world of fashion, that she always dreamt to be there one day.

Since the desire was so strong and she knew her weakness she decided to get into a related field. She must have thought 'so what if I cannot become a model let me get into the cosmetics industry.' She also knew that in those days there was hardly any market for cosmetics for coloured women. She decided to join the sales force of a pharmaceutical company – again distinctly related to cosmetics. See the indirect link? After she gained experience, she got herself a job with the Revlon marketing team. She reached Revlon, but through a different route. Slowly but steadily, she learnt the ropes, listened to her heart, understood the market, and opened her own cosmetics company!

Just imagine being inspired by beautiful models, you start selling pharmaceuticals, and open a cosmetic company. The moral of the story is the most important and practical one. You must keep the fuel of your desire intact, and must use common sense to occupy slots that are best suited to you. Many people go to Mumbai to become actors but after sometime when they realise that acting may not be their best bet, they can well get into direction. Thus, heroes become villains, while many who want to become singers end up becoming good actors instead. Good film directors see the flow of wind, and make films that suit the mood of the masses. They don't go against the current. They simply expand the field of interest.

> Even if you are on the right track, you will get run over if you just sit there.
>
> – *Will Rogers*

• Face your Fears and be Prepared to Take some Risks

Our fears are either internal or external. Learn to face them. If you are prepared to simplify your life, and are prepared to notch down, believe me, 70 per cent of your fears would get taken care of. External fears are usually family pressures, expectations of others, financial commitments, etc. Internal fears are of course, sense of insecurity, fear of failure, and anxiety about success. The greatest internal fear is the fear of what others would think about us. As I said earlier, you must be able to face failure and make a habit to experiment.

What you think about me, is none of my business.

– Anonymous

• Keep an Ear to the Ground and Look for Windows of Opportunities

You may be prepared to take risks, be flexible, conquer your fears, and simplify your life. But you must thereafter look for opportunities. Sitting at home, and doing nothing, will take you nowhere. Look for opportunities, meet people, study the market, and look at others who are doing what you want to do. Once an opportunity comes, strike it hard, and maximise your output.

• Focus

I feel this is one trait which is the most important in every context. If you want to make a mark in your field of interest, then you must keep your eyes firmly fixed on your target. This reminds me of the incident when Arjun was taking an aim at the eye of the fish, and he was asked, 'Arjun what do you see at this point of time?', to which, his answer was, 'I can see only the eye of the fish'. So be focussed.

• Believe in Yourself

Once you are sure of what you want, and are prepared to take risks, then before you get into the fray, you must have faith in yourself.

If a thing is humanly possible, consider it to be within your reach.

– Marcus Aurelius

M.F. Hussain, whose paintings sell today for millions, started his career as a painter of film posters. He developed a style of his own, and made it to the top. He had his share of ups and downs, but he was aware of his talent, and he eventually succeeded (More about M.F. Hussain later.) The bottom line is that, these people loved what they did; for them it is always easy to follow their heart. People who keep their weight in check, often say, 'I eat to live and I don't live to eat'. Similarly, in case of work, I would put it simply like this – I live to work and I don't work to live.

If you go back into history, you would realise that a large number of successful people, at some point of time, were told that they were no good. Those who had faith in themselves and stuck to their guns became very successful. Here are some examples:

Chicken Soup for the Soul series of books, which sold more than 80 million copies, were rejected by 140 major publishing houses, and their agent told the writers that he would not be able to sell the books!

They went door-to-door visiting publishers and eventually found a small publisher, who agreed to push it.

Similarly, at the age of 10, Albert Einstein was told by his teacher, 'You will never amount to much'.

Passion has kept Einstein, Kipling, and Disney going, as they wished to. In fact, passion helps you going against odds, handling setbacks, and criticism.

When Elvis performed in 1954, one of the critics said, 'You aren't going nowhere, son, you got to go back to driving a truck'. Had he acted on the advise of that man, and stopped singing and dancing, the world would have missed out on something great. Elvis sold more than one billion records. Even thirty years after his death he gets more number of hits on 'Google Search' than Tom Cruise and Brad Pit.

When Beatles played in 1962, the recording company said, 'We don't like their sound, and guitars are on the way out anyway'.

So if you have something in your heart that you love to do, please don't suppress and give up. Have faith and continue doing the same.

• Have your own Philosophy to Live Life

It is very natural to draw comparisons. In our day-to-day life, we usually assess and benchmark our success with that of our peers, the guys who went to college with us, who joined the same company, on the same day – which may have been the first day of our jobs. You will always find some of your friends doing better than you – whatever yardstick you follow. Therefore, make a yardstick of your own. If you do do that, you will realise, that at the end of the day, everything evens out. Some have made a lot of money but have health problems. Some have health and wealth but have serious marital problems or their children have not done well. It goes on and on. As long as you are happy, and make a decent living, don't make your life miserable by looking at what others have.

• Be Prepared to take a Setback

When Amitabh Bachchan started his film career, he experienced a number of failures. He almost gave up, but not till his turn came, and he really made it big. He again experienced a setback in his business venture, but bounced back and made a bigger and successful second career. Talented people like him also get rejections, failures, and flops, but they have the courage to fight back the odds.

• Be Prepared for a Change

I talked about flexibility. The other aspect is change. If you are an artist who uses canvasses and oil paints, and it is time to change and go digital, then do so. You must be adaptable, otherwise you would lose the game.

This is like sharpening your axe. Keep learning new techniques, new methods, and always remain abreast with what is happening in your field.

• There is an Opportunity in Every Calamity

When you are pushed too hard, you learn to swim. I have seen some friends who had to leave their jobs because of some misunderstanding with their bosses. They started their own business in the field of their liking, and they succeeded. Many a times when you feel that you have been pushed too hard to the wall, there could always be a chance at that point of time to start something that you wanted to do all along. Consider such setbacks as opportunities, you never know what God has in store for you.

Today, Fields Inc. is a market leader in cookies, and has more than 600 outlets with a multi-million turnover. The owner of this large business, Debbie Fields, has an interesting history. She, in her late teens, got married, and took upon the role of a housewife. At one of the get-togethers, where she had gone with her husband, somebody asked her what was she into. She couldn't give a very satisfactory answer, and the host taunted her at her reply. Debbie felt very humiliated, and took up a challenge to do something worthwhile. She was only good at baking cookies, and she decided to start a business of baking cookies and selling them. Initially she suffered setbacks, but gradually got the business going.

• Don't remain Idealistic, you have to make a Living

Let us not forget that one has to live life – maybe support a family, and even earn a decent living. Therefore, while following your passion, you must keep this hard fact in mind. So, while mapping your drives to professions, you must ensure that you are getting into a profession which can get you a reasonable income. In the Western world, people make money out of unconventional professions, and the same jobs will not get you enough money even to make two ends meet in India. So be realistic, and not totally idealistic. When I said 'notch down', it does not mean you sleep on the railway platform and wear torn clothes. Generally, we go to extremes for earning much money and material, which is unnecessary, and that is what should be kept in mind.

• Don't Over Plan and do Over Research

Sometimes many of us plan more than what is required. In fact, planning is a must, but over planning must be avoided. It is good to be bold, as long as you know it can be done. When John F. Kennedy announced that man will walk on the moon in 10 years, Americans didn't even have the technology! And on 20 July 1969, the first man stood on the Moon. When you commit, you deliver. I would like to mention here that, when you look at successful people who work for passion, they all had the courage to follow these rules.

• Don't get Bogged Down by your Qualifications

Sometimes over-qualification also creates a problem. Keep your mind open, and while aligning your strengths with your passion, don't worry if your qualifications don't match with what you like. During an alumni meet of IIT Bombay, we met some old friends, who were together with us during those days. I met one fellow who had done his electrical engineering, and today he is a top criminal lawyer! I asked him how did this happen. In very simple words, he said that, after graduating from the IIT, he worked for a good MNC for three years, earned a good pay packet, but was not really enjoying the job. So he did his LLB and then LLM, and has been practicing law for more than 15 years. You, therefore, see chartered accountants as successful film directors, mathematics professors turning into great actors, or doctors becoming top cops!

• Expanding the Scope of your Passion – Soul Searching

Here I am going to discuss something very simple, but very practical. According to me, if you use these techniques, you will be able to satisfy your passion, and also make a good living out of it.

First you must write down your drives, your likes or what you love doing. Write it down in precise words. Then think of the profession that would be a direct outcome of this drive. Also, write down how good you are at it. Rate yourself on a count of 10. For example, if acting is my drive, I would write the following.

(a) My drive or passion is acting.

(b) Getting into films is my desire, and I want to become a professional actor.

(c) I am pretty good at it, and I give myself 7 out of 10 (Be realistic here).

Now, you are pretty good at acting, and you are passionate about it. If not films, then what are the related viable professions, where you can deploy your talent and satisfy your drive? Let us divide it into three levels. At the first level are those professions which are directly related to your drive. Second level is the related ones, and the third one is the indirect level. Let us see that, for acting as a drive, what are these possibilities.

Level one: Direct – Acting in films, acting on stage, acting on TV, anchors, radio jockey, master of ceremony, live shows, news readers, concerts, fashion shows, documentary films, ad films.

Level two: Related – Public speaking, high-end training, teaching, mimicry, singing, modelling, advertisements, laughter shows.

Level three: Indirect– Counselling, handling a difficult situation, negotiation, interpersonal communication, politics.

Level three here gives you an idea about how you can use that drive-related skill in different situations. With this analysis, you will be able to expand the scope of your employability. Just imagine that a drive like acting can open up so many windows of opportunity. Adolf Hitler was a great actor, who mesmerised people with his gestures and voice modulation. He used to rehearse for hours before delivering his political speech. It is also important to connect and align your other abilities and drives to your main drive. This would let you expand the scope further, and help you in identifying the best fit. Let us say there is a person who likes to act, and has been on stage as an amateur artist from his school days. He also has a very good sense of humour, and is well-educated in the area of management studies. Corporate mentoring and training can become a very viable profession for such a person.

In most cases, when you restrict your options, you may not get the right opportunities easily. For example, if you have not been able to get into films, then start with stage shows, or try your hand at being a radio jockey. This helps in two ways. It lets you experiment and gain experience, and also gives an opportunity to meet all the people in that profession. You have seen people starting with stage and TV, and getting into films. Shah Rukh Khan is a living example. It is also advisable to try and encash on your strengths. If you look at ghazal singers like Ghulam Ali, Mehndi Hasan, and Jagjit Singh, you would realise that their basic strength lies in classical singing. Using that as a strength, they gave ghazals a different meaning, and simplified it so that the common man can also enjoy it. Had they kept it very complex and stuck to classical singing alone, the public at large would have missed some good music and they wouldn't have reached where they are today. Daler Mehndi was a student of traditional Punjabi music, and learnt it from Raahat Ali Khan Saheb. He became successful only after he switched from classical music to Punjabi Pop.

• Emulating your Heroes

If you play tennis with a better player, you will surely improve your game. You may not get to play with Andre Agassi, but you can always read about him, his style, his strengths, and his success. Obviously, golfers would read about Tiger Woods to get inspiration. When you love something, then I presume that inspiration is already there. Now we have to move beyond inspiration, and get into implementation. At this point of time, looking at these heroes becomes very important.

Therefore, identify a few very successful people in the field or domain that you have chosen to enter. Look up to them as your role models, remote guides, and philosophers. Let me tell you, there is enough written about these guys in articles, books, and biographies. Now worshipping alone is not enough. Remember you have to become like them. Therefore, it makes althemore sense to see how they perform, what makes them tick, and list out all their strengths. Treat them as your domain experts from whom you intend to learn. Do a strength-weakness analysis about each of your domain experts, and make a list.

Now try to match your own strengths and weaknesses with those of these experts. You would realise that these people have great strengths, and you need to make a lot of efforts to come close to them. Let me tell you that these heroes are far from perfect, and you can always find some weaknesses in these successful people. Make sure you don't have these traits in you, so the idea is to 'emulate and improve'. Can you be better than the best? So make a list of what they have and you don't, and also a list of what you have and they don't. In the over-all analysis, you may be as good as any of them. You may also read in general about highly successful people in other domains. For example, Honda and Bill Gates had Napoleon as their hero. In such cases, you get to know the basic winning traits of these people – focus, determination, caring attitude for others, and so on; all of which fall in the domain of emotional intelligence. But when you look at domain experts, you are looking more at their skill-sets, rather than looking at their emotional competence.

During the World War II, the British and Americans generals used to study the habits, behaviours, and strategies of German generals. British and Americans Intelligence used to do proper detailed research, and thereafter prepared thick dossiers on German generals. These were carefully studied by the British and American war commanders, and used extensively to formulate their own war plans! So much so that General Erwin Rommel, the most brilliant general of the German Army, used to drive out of his area and go into the no man's land to look at his own defences! He used to say that looking at your own defences from the adversaries side lets you identify your own weaknesses. Therefore, there is a lot to learn from others. At the end of the chapter, attempt Question 3 and map your strengths and weaknesses with those of your role models.

Making a Switchover

A thought comes to many of us, which makes us ask a simple question: 'Are you living your life the way you wanted to? Or is there something wrong?' These thoughts come at different stages of life, and many a times, for different reasons. You start looking at this major issue during certain periods of life, like attaining the age of 40, or nearing retirement, or even after your annual appraisal.

At certain times, this is triggered because of some external events and calamities, like being a witness to a big train accident, or thousands of people dying during Tsunami. These events shake you up and remind you that life is too short and it can be snuffed out abruptly. That is the time when you sit up and think of a job switch which can let you do what you wanted to do all along.

Sometimes during our days of work, we begin to feel that what we are doing is boring, claustrophobic, and meaningless. It also happens that when you joined a profession or took up a job, things were good, and exciting. As years went by, you realise that the same job is no more exciting, and you feel, 'Oh! I have done it all'. Sometimes, you are forced to think on these lines because of clash of your ethics and values with that of your boss or your organisaton. When you are surrounded by such thoughts, it's time to do an internal check, and see for yourself if you want to make a change or not. For this, the best thing is to take an off or leave for this purpose. Many a times, a sabbatical (many organisaton allow this, which is a long leave given to pursue higher education) can be of a great help. During free time, you can check your problems in a more realistic manner, and it would will help you be in a better position to take a decision.

Getting back the Fizz in your Job

> You don't have to have a reason to feel good — you can feel good for no reason at all.

> — *Jack Penn*

It is quite likely that you don't want to switchover your job as yet, or maybe never, because changing a job is a major decision, and especially when you want to change the profession as well. So be it. You may not be passionate about your current job, and it may not have come out of your passion as such. But there is always room for making your work a little better, peppier, enjoyable, and meaningful. There are more than a dozen practical tips to get some fizz back into your current job. Remember that passion is a self-generated tool.

• Self–Drive and Motivation

There is no substitute for this, and you can always make efforts to motivate yourself. It is not essential to have a great boss and a fantastic organisation to keep yourself motivated. The work itself can give you some joy and pleasure.

• Sense of Achievement and Pride

At the end of the day, you can always look back and say, 'Hey, I achieved so and so', or 'I really did that job very well'. You can always give a pat on your back. Take a bit of pride in what you do. Every soldier in the battlefield is important and contributes to the victory; it is not only the generals who plan the war and get the credit. It is teamwork and in large battle theatres, it is a coordinated show of the army, navy, and the air force.

Your ability to use the principles of auto-suggestion will depend, very largely, upon your capacity to concentrate upon a given desire, until that desire becomes a burning obsession.

— Napoleon Hill

• Involvement

I feel this is one of the most important ways of getting some sense of achievement. If you are in school, get involved with all extracurricular activities. If you are in college, then also get involved in all functions and ceremonies. You need not be at the helm of affairs, but you can always participate. I remember when I wanted to get the library made in my organisation, I engaged an architect, and right from the first design till the implementation phase, I sat with her for every phase of the project – what colours are to be applied, what type of aesthetics, bookshelves, tables, curtains, flooring, etc. are to be used, and so on. I could have, on the other hand, left the entire project to the architect, giving only very initial management directives, and justifying my action by saying, 'The architect is being paid any way'. But this involvement gave me a sense of achievement and getting things done to my satisfaction. I feel getting involved to some extent is an inborn trait, but to a large extent it can be developed by making a conscious effort.

• Creativity

Now you don't have to be Pablo Picasso to be creative. You can always use your creative side in your daily work. Even organising a small birthday party within the office for your colleague, can always demonstrate creativity. This is an important aspect which is discussed later in the book. I used my creative sense while getting the library done.

• Innovation

Linked very close to creativity, is innovation. It simply means getting jobs done in a different style. Innovation keeps you alive, and also gets you that badly needed sense of self-esteem and satisfaction.

• Making Work into a Hobby

This is a matter of perception. Why do you want to make hobby into a work, and why not make work into a hobby?

• Be the Best

Develop competitive feelings within you. I am sure there are many of you working in a team or in a large organisation to generate a healthy competition. Don't have that, 'I also ran' attitude. Try to see that you perform better than others. You may take on a couple of your coworkers to start with, and mentally try and see that you perform better than them; and then increase the radius to be better than most. One day you'll be the best.

• I Must Give Value for Money

Each one of us has a conscience. Make sure you don't go against it. Your organisation is paying you for your work, so you must give it back its value for money. Always remember, nobody employs you for charity, and why should you live on somebody's charity? So pay back in terms of work, and you will feel that sense of pride.

• Making Friends

This is a great stress buster, which helps you to get rid of those Monday morning blues, because you are not only going for work, you are also going to meet some good friends out there. It would also help you in sharpening your interpersonal skills. In every organisation you have a variety of choice as far as making friends is concerned. Do you know that a five star hotel has more than 500 employees! Can you have difficulty in making five good friends with whom you can spend time during lunch, or coffee/ tea breaks? Oh yes, you can easily do it.

• Learn New Things

Organisations facilitate learning and development, and every job gives you enough opportunities to learn. Make sure you avail all of such opportunities like seminars, workshops, and training programmes. In addition, you can always make efforts to pick up new skills, as on-the-job learning, maybe from your colleagues as well. In this way, you sharpen your axe regularly, and keep yourself happily occupied.

• Get into a Teaching Mode – Share your Experiences

You acquire special skills while you are doing your day-to-day jobs. Look for opportunities where universities and colleges invite visiting faculties to deliver lectures on special subjects or conduct workshops. For example, if you are into marketing of services, and have a good experience in marketing service solutions, you will be able to teach your subject to fresh graduates quite well. For this, you will have to read a little, collect your thoughts together, and make a decent presentation. This will get you involved not only in the presentation, but also in your job. At the end of it, you would have gone back to your college days feeling younger and more energetic. Let me tell you, this gives a tremendous amount of satisfaction. It also adds to your self-esteem.

• Try to Help Others solve their Problems

If you adopt a helpful attitude to help your colleagues in solving their job-related problems, you will get a sense of satisfaction and achievement. You also generate goodwill, improve your interpersonal relations, and make more friends at the workplace.

• Set some Goals for Yourself

Many a times when you start drifting into boredom in your job, you feel you are getting deeper and deeper into quick sand. To pull yourself out of a negative spiral, it is important to set some sort of goals for yourself. These goals have to be related to your job, and not to your personal goals. Simple day-to-day, and weekly targets, get you going. Achieving these simple goals also give you a sense of achievement and self-worth.

• Imagine where you would be Five Years down the Line in the Same Profession

If viewed positively, this can be a moral booster. You can think of some promotional avenues, more challenging assignments, new projects, or a change of location or job. All this keeps the adrenaline flowing in your blood, and keeps you pepped up.

• Change the Context of your Work

Now this is easier said than done. But I will illustrate it with a simple example. You have your lunch everyday on the dining table, at home or at your workplace. On a Sunday, you prepare lunch, pack it in a nice basket, and put into the boot of your car. You drive 30 kilometers, go outside the town, look for a tree on the hill top, walk up all the way, open the basket, and have your lunch while looking down at some lake! And this is picnic for you. This is change of context in simple terms. Be innovative, and see how you can give a different meaning, and a different context to your mundane day-to-day work. Enjoy the picnic.

Let your Passion remain alive: Professional or Not

It may well happen that you have a passion, and you also have talent and capability. But you are happy with your job and do not wish to make any change in your smoothly-running life. Good enough. It is not necessary to make a hobby into a profession, and in certain cases, it may not work out to be a viable (financially viable) deal. But one thing is certain, that you should never let your passion whither away or die down. As a hobby, it works as a great stress buster, and gives you some fun and satisfaction, if not money. You never know you may get an opportunity to connect your passion with a money-making activity, which can one day become a full-time profession.

I know a person who has done his Masters in Business Administration, and was working as a well-paid executive in a large company. He was also acting as an anchor for stage shows as a hobby. One odd show in a month would help him earn an extra buck, and give him the satisfaction of being on the stage. In one of these stage shows, he was spotted by the CEO of a very prestigious company and was offered an excellent job of a senior executive. That company utilised his professional abilities as well as his talent.

There are various ways of keeping in touch with the things that you like. Here are few examples:

• For Musicians

Gifted musicians can play with a local music club, form their own amateur group, play at charity concerts, or even do their own recording and make their own CDs, which can be given to friends. Today, there are a number of TV shows which provide a platform to launch budding artists.

• For Artists

Artists can paint sufficient number of paintings, or what they are good at, and can hold a small exhibition at a rented place, a restaurant, or a fair.

• For Speakers

Speakers can hold talk shows at clubs, like Rotary or Lions, professional organisations, and so on. They can also try their hands being a radio jockey.

• For Actors

Actors can join some amateur group, try street plays, and so on. Later they can try their hands at TV serials.

• For Writers

Writing is a pleasure for writers. Of course getting it published is also very important. Writers should write on the subject that they like. Today, there are number of magazines and newspapers available in the market. The rejection rate in good newspapers is very high, but if you are good you will surely get noticed.

Test Drive your Hobby

To understand the difference between liking something and wanting to perform, it could be difficult with most of the people. It is important to realise that you enjoy performing that activity, or are you in love with the name alone? To discover this the best way is to pursue that as a hobby, as explained earlier. It would also be helpful if you can volunteer to do some free work or charity. So first perform for free, and then decide whether you like the work or not.

If you are planning to buy a new motorbike, you go and try out at least five different brands with numerous versions and models. Before buying a motorbike you research from automobile magazines, talk to the people who purchased latest models, and also go for a test drive. Remember test drives are free, and you burn the fuel at the cost of the showroom!

First of all, decide to try your hobby for about 80 hours, i.e., experimenting for about 10 days, at the rate of 8 hours a day. This could be done during vacations at a stretch, or during weekends. Volunteered work must be done at two or three different levels and perform as many roles as possible. You may realise that it is not as good as you thought, or it may be better than what you expected. Remember, the taste of the pudding is in its eating! And even while writing your resume, you must write this as your work experience, and not as a hobby or extracurricular activity. This way, it will give serious signal to the prospective employer.

Lets us Recapitulate

- A large number of small businesses are based on hobbies. People who are into occupations that are motivated by creativity are into it because of passion.

- Thumb rules to live your passion
    - ◊ Be prepared to notch down
    - ◊ Simplify your life
    - ◊ Be flexible
    - ◊ Face your fears, and be prepared to take some risks
    - ◊ Keep an ear to the ground, and look for windows of opportunities
    - ◊ Focus
    - ◊ Believe in yourself
    - ◊ Have your own Philosophy to live life
    - ◊ Be prepared to take a setback
    - ◊ Be prepared for a change

◊   There is an opportunity in every calamity

◊   Don't remain idealistic; you have to make a living

◊   Don't over-plan or over-research

◊   Don't get bogged down by your qualifications.

- Expand the scope of your passion

You must align your strengths with what you love. Try to see in what different fields you can apply your drive, which can culminate into a viable profession.

- Making a Switchover

You must take sometime out for yourself, so that you can take a decision to make a job switch.

- Emulate your Heroes

You must identify a few role models who have excelled in the domain of your liking. Study their strengths and styles. Learn from their strategies and techniques. Get inspired by them and keeping them as benchmark, make efforts to improve your performance.

- Getting back that Fizz in your Job

    ◊   Self-drive and motivation

    ◊   Sense of achievement and pride

    ◊   Involvement

    ◊   Creativity

    ◊   Innovation

    ◊   Changing work into a hobby

    ◊   Be the best

    ◊   I must give value for money

    ◊   Making friends

    ◊   Learn new things

    ◊   Get into a teaching mode – share your experiences

    ◊   Try to help others solve their problems

◊ Set some goals for yourself

◊ Imagine where you would be five years down the line in the same profession

◊ Change the context of your work

◊ Let your passion remain alive: professional or not

YOUR PERSONAL ROAD MAP

1. Check your ability to apply passion.

    (a) Are you prepared to notch down a little in order to follow your passion?

    (b) Does your family support you on this?

    (c) Are you prepared to simplify your life?

    (d) Are you prepared to be flexible when you want to do something related to your passion?

    (e) Are you prepared to take a little risk? Do you believe in yourself?

    (g) Are you prepared to change and sharpen your axe?

    These questions will let you think about how serious you are about following your passion, and changing it into a career.

2. Exercise to expand the scope of your drive

    (a) Write down what drives you.

    (b) How good are you at it? Rate yourself out of 10.

    (c) Now write the professions that can emanate out of this drive in three levels:

    Direct

    Related

    Indirect

    Now try to choose those which are within your reach.

3. Write down the names of three people who have done very well in the field that you wish to choose. Study their profiles

by reading books and articles, and list out their strengths and weaknesses. Now try to match your strengths and weaknesses.

                        My Hero   And Me

(a) Skills
     (Vary from domain to domain)

(b) Emotional Competence
     (Suggested List)
     * Attitude
     * Commitment
     * Beliefs/Values
     * Fighting Spirit
     * Patience
     * Dedication
     * Perseverance
     * Integrally

(c) Major decisions taken during their lifetime

(d) Strategies

(e) Special Strengths
     (Vary from person-to-person)

(f) History
     * Childhood
     * Schooling
     * Education/Training
     * Early days of career
     * Getting in the success zone
     * Any other

The true mark of intelligence is the ability to hold two opposing ideas in the mind simultaneously.

                                         – *F. Scott Fitzgerald*

4

Those Madly Passionate People

Follow the Leaders

Gravity can't be held responsible for falling in love.

- Albert Einstein

In this chapter, I would like to write about those people who have demonstrated success in some field or the other. Common sense tells us that these people couldn't have been successful, and continued in that field for so long without liking it, if not loving it. Therefore, it would not be wrong to say that all the successful people love their work. Passion and love for work is universal, therefore, I would like to share examples from the domestic as well as international scenario. I would also like to draw some lessons from these success stories.

What gives you a high or a kick is not confined only to fine arts, photography, or music. It could be just about anything. Achieving excellence itself is a thrill for many. Beating competition, customer satisfaction, building a car from the scratch, could all be very satisfying activities. I would like to mention here that passion alone is not enough to ensure success. You need to connect it with your strengths and make it a viable proposition; a workable profession. It would be foolish to follow what you love passionately, and end up like a pauper. As we proceed, you would realise the power of diversification. In other words, proliferating your preferences into as many related activities or professions, is the key to success. In most cases, gifted people find a purpose in what they do, and eventually, all of them who succeed, demonstrate a serious degree of perseverance. Therefore, anybody with talent and passion who has failed to be successful, would have fallen short in terms of perseverance, or to some extent, failing to find a purpose. Now let us look at some of those who made it big. I have taken examples of people from music, business, and many other fields, because passion and success are applicable across the domains. 'Reading a story is knowledge, but the moral of the story is wisdom.' Therefore, don't concentrate too much on the stories, but do note carefully the learnings which have been summarised at the end of each story. Learn from their zeal, dedication, and other traits, which made them stand apart.

SUNIL BHARTI MITTTAL

Ambitious, Compassionate, and an Entrepreneur at Heart

This man from Ludhiana, a graduate from Punjab University, started a small bicycle parts manufacturing business in 1976 with about Rs 20,000. He tried his hand at hosiery and steel utensils as well. Being mediocre in studies, he chose to pursue business as a profession, and a source of livelihood. Today, he is the chairman of the US$2.7 billion worth Bharti Enterprise. This man is passionate about his work, always wants to try new things, and is in a hurry. Therefore, speed, innovation, and passion are his drivers. When asked what gives him a high, he replied very candidly in one of his interviews, and said, 'if you are asking me what's your kick, then I would say size is what gives me a thrill. Building a large company is what I long for'. He also says that it is difficult to understand what gives anybody a kick, 'can somebody tell me why women get fascinated by diamonds? And why a fat ugly looking lady be bothered about a big diamond?' he asks.

There is, therefore, an unexplained affinity for diamonds, he says, and he also can't understand why people are crazy about their gardens, or for their Armani clothes, or about restaurants, and so on. Therefore, he says people don't understand why he works 18 hours a day, mostly till midnight in his office. That is, he says, is his kick. To start a business with US$800 and build a business empire of over US$ 1 billion in about two decades, is what gives him a high. He looks forward to coming to the office everyday, and it is not for money, because he has made enough to last three generations, and to live like a king.

He explains his enthusiasm and involvement by giving an example. Mantra was the ISP launched by the Bharti Group, and Satyam Infoway was launched by Satyam. Although successful, Mantra was not as successful as Satyam Infoway. The reason is that, Sunil Mittal couldn't plunge himself into ISP business, as he could, for Airtel. He couldn't give his 100 per cent to the two ventures at the same time. Therefore, total involvement and passion are very important for any business.

He again takes the example of Mantra to express his views about passion and success. He says that, had he put all his energy behind Mantra and done nothing else, he would have taken it to the top! He thus says, stimulation is to be 'cloned' by having a few highly passionate people who can run the business. He says that, success is in concentrating on one thing, and that means focus. He also says that, if you keep looking at nice orchards outside your field, then you would tend to focus. So when he wakes up in the morning he doesn't have to say,

'My God, what do I do with my steel plant!' He says he doesn't get distracted, because he sticks to telecom which is his passion and core competence.

Sunil Mittal's romance with telecom started first with push-button telephones in 1985–86. It was his first fight with the 'big boys' who were large cash-rich companies. He quotes Mahatma Gandhi, who said, 'first they ignore you, then they laugh at you, and then they fight you'. Sunil Mittal fought these big competitions at all the three stages, and emerged as a winner.

He not only advocates passion for work, but also believes in compassion for people who work for Bharti. He goes on to say, 'I do not believe in Jack Welch and his concept of forced ranking – eliminating 10 per cent of employees every year. We are wedded to the cause and not the business'. Well said Mr Mittal.

Moral of the Story of Sunil Mittal

- Passion is an unexplained phenomenon – it could be for diamonds, food, excellence, money, or just playing big.

- Enthusiasm and focus are very important for success. You should play within your own core competence.

- Think big and it can be done. From cycle parts to steel utensils, and to being one of the largest telecom players, is a possibility. Thinking big and creating something big can also give you a high.

- A graduate from Punjab University showed that you don't have to worry much about qualifications.

- It requires perseverance and hard work to be successful.

- Passionate people don't work for money; they work because they like taking challenges.

It seemed to me pretty plain that they had more of love than matrimony.

– Oliver Gridsmith

SABEER BHATIA

Inventor, Innovator, and an Entrepreneur

As an excellent and intelligent student, Sabeer Bhatia did his schooling from Pune, and went on to do his engineering from Birla Institute of Technology – BITS Pilani. While at BITS, he applied for the Cal Tech scholarship which is extremely difficult to get, and was the only applicant in the entire world in 1988 to achieve a score of 62, with the next highest score being 42! He did his bachelors and then masters in electrical engineering from Stanford University, registered for PhD, and dropped soon after to join Apple Computers as a Systems Integrator.

He was just 19 when he reached America with only $ 250 in his pocket, and by the time he was 31, just 12 years later, the man was worth the US $ 400 million! With the brain of a techie, and the heart of a businessman, Sabeer Bhatia made all his money and got all the success with one great idea. Love for his work and smooth implementation of his business plan. He had that entrepreneurial drive from his childhood, and even in school he would think of setting up a sandwich stall.

He had a raw idea of a free email on the internet, and a big dream to get it going. About his success he says, 'It is a story of passion, we started a small company in a two-room office with a big idea, had fun building it, never realising that it would turn out so big'. His favourite story is about the initial approach to venture capitalists in Silicon Valley, to obtain funding for his venture. They had named it 'Hot Mail', and each time he called up and mentioned the idea, he would end up listening to giggles of the secretaries of the senior executives he was calling – they thought he was trying to set up a pornographic site called 'Hot Male'. After 19 rejection's, he could manage to get the money.

Hotmail was launched on 4 July 1996, and got 100 subscribers within an hour. By mid 1998 the company was getting 1.25 lakhs subscribers per day! He had built a customer base faster than any media company in history – beating CNN and America online, hands down.

Bill Gates got interested, and by the time Microsoft approached him, his customer base had reached 60 lakhs. Sabeer bid half a billion dollars for Hotmail, and after a number of rounds of fierce negotiations, sold it to Microsoft for US$ 400 million – what a reward for immense hard work had gone into building the venture! This could well-afford him a 3,000 sq ft apartment in Pacific Heights, a BMW, and a Ferrari. A risk-taker, Sabeer talks about his gambling instincts and says, 'The best piece of advise someone gave me was that the biggest risk in life is not to take risk at all.' To wrap it up he says, 'In the long run, it boils down to a simple fact – how much faith does one have in oneself'. One of his friends, Farouk Arjani, says about him, 'What really set Sabeer apart, from hundreds of entrepreneurs I have met, is the gargantuan size of his dream'.

Moral of the Story of Sabeer Bhatia

- Be prepared to take some risks.
- Have confidence in yourself. This also means you got to have solid stuff in you, if you want to succeed in your field.
- Passion for work is very important.
- Negotiate for the price if your stuff is good. Somebody will pay for it.
- Listen to your gut feeling.

- Connecting your strengths is very important. In his case, it was technology and his business sense.

I am for an art that is political – erotical – mystical, that does something other than sit on its ass in a museum.

– Claes Oldenburg

M F Hussain

He Observes the World with a Child's Eyes

Maqbool Fida Hussain, the 90 year old maverick painter created history in the Indian art with the headlines, 'M F Hussain's paintings to fetch Rs 300 crore via auction!' The occasion was the auction of a series of 100 paintings entitled 'Our Planet called Earth'.

At the age of 20, somewhere in the 1935, Hussain came to Mumbai and got admitted to the J J School of Arts. Since there were not many takers for art those days, he earned money painting cinema hoardings. He says 'We were paid four annas per square foot and for a 6 × 10 feet canvas we got a few rupees.'

In addition he designed and made toys for some toy factory. Gradually, he started making paintings and participating in exhibitions. Around the 1960s his work got recognition and in 1966 he was awarded the Padmashree by the Government of India. He being an artist tried his hand at cinema and made his first film 'Through the eyes of a Painter' which was shown at the Berlin film festival and won a Golden Bear. Later he became a public figure and also got into many controversies which has been going on till date. He gave public performances by making paintings in front of a crowd for several days–and finally, on the last day destroyed his own paintings by over painting with the white colour! His most popular paintings are of horses and abstract themes. His murals are simply out of the world.

This self–styled artist – was awarded Padma Bhushan in 1973, Padma Vibhushan in 1989 and was nominated to the Rajya Sabha in 1986. He defies age by thinking young and experimenting new forms of art. He has never been a conformist and has painted what he liked and painted the way he wanted to paint. He has experimented with different medias like canvas, murals as well as celluloid. When he was asked about the secret of his speed and success, he very humbly said that it is the gift of the God. He went on to say 'To me each day unfolds like a magic box, full of surprises. I am always interested in everything I perceive and I observe the world with a childs eyes.' Totally confident about his abilities he says I have always been the master of my art.' And he has recently painted 'Vision! The 20th Century' which chronicles the moods, events and personalities of the last century.

Anyone who says he can't see a thought simply doesn't know art.

— *Wynetka Ann Reynolds*

Moral of the Story of M F Hussain

- If you have a God's gift, never let it go waste.
- With God's gift you need perseverance.
- To stand out in the world, you got to be different.
- If you have passion, then money is a by-product you can move from Rs 15 a painting to Rs 100 crores.
- Diversify your talent into different areas, and be prepared for experimenting – paintings, murals, and films, in his case.
- Don't worry what others think about you.

The buttocks are the most aesthetically pleasing part of the body because they are non functional. Although they conceal an essential orifice, these pointless globes are as near as human form can ever come to abstract art.

— *Kenneth Tynan*

NARAYANA MURTHY

Values, Sweat Equity, and Compassion

As a chairman and head of Infosys, this man needs no introduction. Starting his entrepreneurial career in 1981 with money borrowed from his wife, he along with some of his other friends, started Infosys. Narayana Murthy, whose role models have been his parents and teachers, has kept his childhood learnings very close to his heart. Simple but rock-solid principles, like values, honesty, hard work, compassion, and respect for talent, are his guiding force.

Having cleared his IIT entrance exam, he had to join a local engineering college, because his father could not afford the high fees at IIT! Narayana Murthy later went to IIT Kanpur to do his masters, and it is there that he was introduced to computers, and got hooked. He then went on to serve as a chief systems programmer at IIM Ahmedabad, where he learnt his ropes and acquired a solid knowledge base. However, his salary – Rs 800 a month – a pittance. It is here that he came in contact with Professor Krishnayya, and learnt from him how important it is to 'aspire' and to learn. Working in a charged-up atmosphere for about 20 hours a day, laid his technical foundation. He learnt from every opportunity, every event, every competitor, and all his colleagues. He is of the opinion that, to distribute wealth, you must create wealth – else you will be distributing poverty. Participating in a huge number of social activities, he is a compassionate capitalist at heart. He is always grateful to God and life for being kind to him, and providing the right opportunities at the right time.

Nine years after its launch in 1990, Infosys went through a very bad phase. They were even contemplating a shut down or a sell out. But they discussed the matter and decided against it, and restarted their marathon race. It was he who inspired the team to hold on. He very aptly puts that, leadership is about making what seems impossible, and changing the perception of your team. As he says, chance favours the prepared mind, and in 1991, the liberalisation process in India did the same for Infosys. He also gives credit to his habit of introspection, which he has not only restricted as a personal habit, but has also made it as an organisational culture. He calls it his best business decision. He believes in trust and in value systems like the British Constitution, which is unwritten, but is well-practiced. He says that it is better to lose a billion dollars than a good night sleep.

> Business is like a man rowing a boat upstream. He has no choice, he must go ahead, or he will go back.
>
> *– Lewis E Pierson*

To him money really doesn't matter much. A man of simple habits who has his feet firmly on ground, he says that beyond a certain comfort level, wealth should be seen as an opportunity to make a difference to the society. He feels that 'Power of Money is the Power to Give'. He also advises the next generation, that it is good to go early to bed and rise early, which works wonders. Get a marketable idea, and understand the windows of opportunity for it. Entrepreneurship is about running a marathon, and not a 100 m sprint. On what drives him, he says that the reward for winning a pinball game is to get a chance to play the next one. It is not the destination, but the journey which gives you pleasure.

> Business is like a game of tennis – those who serve will usually end up winning.
>
> *– Anonymous*

Moral of the Story of Narayana Murthy

- Basic values are as important for organisations as they are for individuals, to achieve success.

- You can find your passion at any time of your life. He got hooked to computers at IIT Kanpur, and had no clue about it before.

- If you like something, just do it, don't worry about the money. Remember he took up his first job for Rs 800 per month. Money comes on its own, and that too in volumes!

- Be thankful to God for providing you with opportunities.

- Don't give up, and have faith in yourself and be prepared. Chance always favours the prepared.

- Introspection is essential at an individual, as well as organisational level.

- Getting the best team, and respecting and rewarding the people who work for you, is extremely important.

- Never compromise on your values, whatever be the bait.

- You may have talent, but you must get a marketable idea, and then back it with hardwork.

- You must always aspire and be willing to learn.

- It's not the destination, but the journey, which gives you pleasure. People with passion do it because they love doing it.

  Our passions are the time phoenixes; when the old one is burnt out, a new one rises from the ashes.

  – Johanna Goethe

SUBHASH CHANDRA

Observe, Identify, Experiment, and Diversify

His mantra for success is, 'One should not be overjoyed by too much success, and not get depressed if one fails. Keep doing your Karma'. This man who wanted to become an engineer like most people those days – dropped out of Class 12, and started his own vegetable oil business at the age of 19, and within a few years, took his company turnover to US$ 12.5 million. His simple idea of storing food grains in the open, and covering with polythene sheets, worked miracles for Food Corporation of India in 1976. The same year, he ventured into the export of food grains, and made good profits. He touches the untouched areas, often generating new ideas, and making them successful. His strength is in observation, identifying a window of opportunity, and execution. Also, he practises his business principle, 'No backing off even in the face of losses', to the hilt.

In 1981, during a visit to a packaging exhibition, he came up with an innovative packaging idea of manufacturing integrated multilayered laminated tubes, as a substitute to aluminium tubes, used by FMCG companies like dental care, pharma, and cosmetics. It has risen to manufacturing capacity of 3 billion tubes, with a market capitalisation of the US$125 million. Today, it holds the number one position in laminated tube manufacturing. His visit to amusement parks abroad, promoted him to start Asia's largest amusement park Essel World. Known as the media Czar, his getting into the broadcasting business was also due to a chance visit to meet a friend at the Mumbai Doordarshan office, in the early 1990s. Just two years later, he started Zee TV in October 1992. He had no knowledge of technology or distribution, but he was inquisitive to learn. Within a short span of time, he started other channels, and this bouquet of channels came under the umbrella of Zee Network. On a single day Zee Network reaches out to more than 32 million households across India, and has its reach spanning USA, Caribbean, the Middle East, Europe, Africa, Far East, Australia, and New Zealand! For his Zee TV ventures, he was backed by some foreign investors to bring private satellite television channels to India.

His latest venture was to start an online lottery – again the first of its type in the country. His company is engaged in building more than a dozen family entertainment centres across

India, that would have multiplexes, food courts, bowling alleys shopping malls, and lots of other options. From vegetable oil to food grains, from packing to amusement parks, from satellite network to online lottery, and to entertainment centres, has been quite a journey. Standing today as India's third most powerful billionaire, is quite an achievement.

Moral of the Story of Subhash Chandra

- His drive is to get into untouched fields, learn about them, and make them a success.

- Look for windows of opportunity. Observe, and then implement.

- Curiosity is the key to diversification.

- Do your best and don't clamour for rewards.

- Common sense is more important than formal education.

- If you have good ideas, you will get the support of others.

- Honesty, and a clean business dealing, pays in the long run.

> I don't know anything about music. In my line you don't have to.
>
> *– Elvis Presley*

A R Rahman

Musical Magic in his fingers

Born actually as A S Dileep Kumar in the year 1966, A R Rahman, in a short span of time, has revolutionalised the Indian music. His father, R K Shekhar, was a composer in Malayalam movies, and had worked with people like Salil Choudhary. A R Rahman had displayed musical prowess since his childhood, and played piano and harmonium from the age of four. One day, a music director friend of his father saw this four year old playing the harmonium. He covered the keyboard with a cloth, but it made no difference – Dileep replayed the tune effortlessly.

In his heart of hearts, he wanted to become an electronic or a computer engineer, and was more interested in technology. He was first attracted towards music when his father got a synthesiser for him from Singapore. In a family, where music was all around, he viewed it more as a means of livelihood than passion. But this one gift from his father was to change his life forever, since it was an ideal combination of music and technology.

He lost his father when he was nine years old, and his belief in God took a beating at that point of time. For the survival of family, he joined a troupe as a keyboard player, and formally entered the world of music as a professional. In between, he played for orchestras, and later, even accompanied the tabla wizard, Zakir Hussain on world tours. He tried his hand at composing music for a few regional films. Playing with different people, and some of them of great repute, he learnt a lot about music quite early in life. This earned him a scholarship to the Trinity College of Music at Oxford University, from where he got his degree in Western Classical Music.

He came back to India and gave a contemporary and international flavour to the Indian music. He still performed with some rock bands, worked with some music directors, and gradually music became the only source of joy to him. He found that working with music directors and playing the same thing again and again with rock bands, was suppressing his creativity. He wanted to do something different. On someone's suggestion, he went into composing short jingles for advertisements, and in a period of just five years composed more than 300 jingles. This also gave him exposure to the film industry. His popular ads were for Airtel, Titan, MRF, and Asian Paints, to name a few.

Music is the art of thinking with sounds.

– Jules Combarieu

Due to some personal reasons, the family took to Islam, and he, from Dileep Kumar, became Allah Rakha Rahman. He feels that he inherited enormous knowledge of music from his father, and calls it the grace of God. He also gives credit to working for ad films and jingles, which give precision and sense of timing for his music. He says, that in jingles, you only have a few seconds to create a mood or convey an emotion or give a message. It also teaches you discipline and rigour.

Mani Ratnam, the famous film director, met him at an advertising awards function, and A R Rahman got a chance to play a few of his tunes, for him. He liked them so much, that he signed him for his film *Roja* that was released in 1992. A R Rahman hit the bull's eye, and composed such a different music, which established him as a music director with a difference. Rest is as they say history, and he gave musical scores in films like *Taal*, *Rangeela*, *Zubeda* and *Lagaan* to name a few. Today, he has carved a niche for himself, and made a style of his own.

Moral of the Story of A R Rahman

- You may be gifted, but initially in life, you may have your interests in areas other than the gifted domain.

- Despite the inherited competence, you got to work hard, try your hand at all the related fields, learn from others, and then only you can be successful.

- You can get into passion while doing a job.

- Slow and steady wins the race.

- You must meet and experiment with as many people as possible, because you learn from each of them.

- If you are good, you will make it to the top one day.

  Music is the only language in which you cannot say mean or sarcastic things.

  – Lord Erskine

KALPANA CHAWLA

Inspired by Small Little Things

This lady from a middle-class family in India, did her country proud. She was part of a seven member crew aboard space shuttle Columbia, which having spent 16 days in space, exploded in the atmosphere, just 16 minutes before the touch down. This was Kalpana's second flight to space.

From her childhood, she was different from her peers and as a young girl was happier painting and sketching airplanes rather than playing with dolls. When asked what put her on the road to NASA, and how she got into this, her answers were straight and candid. She was always fascinated by the air planes flying overhead in the little town in India where she lived. On her request, her father took her to the flying club to get her a ride in the Pushpak training aircraft. Some of these very simple things helped her in making her mind to get into aerospace engineering.

Being good in studies served as a plus point, and she could get the subjects of her choice in school, which enabled her to get into aerospace engineering course. At that point of time, she was keen on becoming a flight engineer, but also wanted to design an aircraft, which was an entirely different job. You have passion, but may not have clarity of thought. She, in her interview, once said that, she has no idea as to what a flight engineer did, and of course, of course she didn't have the remotest idea that she would get into this. Her inspiration came from people in all walks of life. She was also inspired by people like J R D Tata, who had made their mark in the Indian aviation history. She would get inspired by anyone who went out of the way to do something. Her teachers in school were a source of inspiration for her, because of their efforts to teach and encourage students to study. She was also inspired by explorers and people who went for adventure.

Courage is being scared to death — but saddling anyway.

— John Wayne

Reading books about adventure,daring feats, and perseverance, was a great source of inspiration for Kalpana Chawla. She had a brilliant academic record, and took part in almost everything, from athletics, dance, and sports, to science, and modelling. She enjoyed flying, backpacking, hiking, and reading. Her general passion quotient was very high. An avid pilot, she had a flight instructor's license, and also a commercial pilot's license for single and multi-engines land and sea planes. She did her MS in aerospace engineering, and later got a PhD in the same discipline. Kalpana was selected out of 2,000 applicants for civilian scientists post for being onboard Columbia's voyage. Intense physical fitness, academic achievements, and flying experience as a pilot, made her a natural choice for the space shuttle, Columbia.

Moral of the Story of Kalpana Chawla

- Inspiration can come from very simple things.

- You must align your other abilities, along with your passion, to become successful.

- There are people who are self-motivated and draw motivation from successful and motivated people.

- A strong desire to achieve a goal is all that is required to achieve it.

- Strong determination is required, along with the desire for your ultimate success.

I have no special gift — I am only passionately curious.

– Albert Einstein

THOMAS EDISON

A Curious Child, Scientist, An Inventor, and an Industrialist

From the age of about four years, Thomas Edison was a curious child, who would plead with every adult he met to explain the working of just about everything he encountered. Modern psychology would have labelled him a victim of Attention Deficit Syndrome, because of his habit of questioning almost everything. Apart from having a scientific bent of mind, he loved Shakespeare and reciting poetry.

He was introduced to a local library by his parents for good reading habits. This made him into an independent learner who could dig out answers for himself, making him into a young scientist and an inventor at heart. His mother encouraged him to learn, and was very sure of his special abilities. This boy had a passion to learn and invent. A poor student at school, he was a child who taught himself much by reading on his own. He believed in self-improvement, and this remained throughout his life. Thomas Edison, throughout his life, relentlessly worked to invent things, that would improve the quality of life on Earth. He got 1,093 patents in his 84 years of life, and never stopped coming up with new ideas.

The charm of courage is that they are inventions, inspirations, flashes of genius.

– R W Emerson

He believed in hard work, and had a capacity to work for 20 hours a day. His famous quote is Genius is 1 per cent inspiration and 99 per cent perspiration.

His first legitimate invention was an electric vote recording machine, which turned out to be a disaster, because probably it was ahead of its time, and there were no takers for it. From this, he learnt a lesson that, 'never to waste time inventing things that people would not want to buy.' Most famous for the invention of light bulb, he had also been the inventor of phonograph, a recording machine, which could record and reproduce sound, and a motion picture camera which recorded and reproduced moving pictures. These three inventions alone were the most important discoveries of the century. Light, sound, camera, and action followed.

The success of light bulb and his inventions brought him name, fame, and money. He, in a way, founded the electric industry, and spent a large part of his effort making a reliable centralised generation, efficient distribution system, and a successful end use (electric bulb). He founded the Edison General Electric, with a large number of generating plants across the world – later to be known as only general electric or GE.

He invested his own money for inventions, and many of his experiments and inventions failed, and he lost a lot of money in such ventures. But an inventor at heart is always an inventor at heart – and this spirit made him experiment in diverse areas like cement and mining iron ore! Edison had his hands in almost every pie, and was more responsible than anyone else for creating the modern world. No one did more to shape the physical meke-up of the present-day present day civilisation, and therefore, he was the most influential figure of the last millennium. Curious to learn, ready to invent, and totally involved, he was a one-man invention industry. To pay tribute to this man who lit the world, lights in the United States were dimmed for one minute on 21 October 1931, a few days after his death.

> The first requisite for success is the ability to apply your physical and mental energies to one problem incessantly, without growing weary.
>
> *– Thomas Edison*

Moral of the Story of Thomas Edison

- Curiosity could be the biggest gift of God.

- If you want to be more successful, then you must proliferate your strengths and passion within your domain. He got 1,093 patents in different areas during his lifetime.

- Always deploy your skills, and drive in such a way, that you can come up with 'marketable' outputs. There is no point of putting efforts in areas where there will be no takers for your products. It is equally applicable to inventions, music, art, poetry, books, articles, and so on.

- Don't sit in an ivory tower and invent things that nobody wants.

- Diversify, and be prepared to take a little risk.

- Passion must be backed with hard work, if you want to be successful.

- You must develop reading habits. In fact, earmark sometime for reading. At home, inculcate this habit in children, which will go a long way in making them successful.

- Children should be encouraged and given access to books which are related to their passion.

To be a great champion you must believe you are the best. If you are not, pretend you are.

– Muhammad Ali

MUHAMMAD ALI

Passionate, Focused, Determined to Win

Cassius Clay, popularly known as Muhammad Ali, had a childhood dream of becoming a boxing champion. 12-year old Cassius Clay got into boxing when his bike got stolen. He told the policeman that he wanted to bash up the thief. Looking at this young boy, the policeman suggested him to prepare well, and learn boxing before facing the thief. He took this so seriously that he joined the training with Fred Stoner. The rest is history. There are very few people in the history of sports who have achieved what Ali could. He was so enthusiastic about the game and winning every bout, that he worked his way up to be the world heavyweight boxing champion, thrice.

His winning spree started when he was under 18, and was still under training with more than one hundred amateur boxing sessions under his belt. He was so focused, dedicated, and involved, that he never took to any other job than training himself for boxing! His drive was victory, and his passion was to be in the ring. He won his gold medal in the light heavyweight category in 1960 at the Olympics in Rome. Within years, he turned professional. In 1964, he knocked down Sonny Liston, and became the world's heavyweight boxing champion.

He developed a new style of boxing for himself. He tried to remain out of the opponent's reach – to avoid being hit. Another style was 'dancing in the ring', for which he developed his own rhythm, and used to shuffle everywhere inside the ring. His legs were very powerful – maybe the strongest in the history of boxing, which made him literally float in the ring. This became famous as the 'Ali Shuffle'. He had tremendous confidence, very powerful punch, and an equally big mouth. He never used to mince words. In a time when boxers never talked to media, Ali used to do all the talking. His most famous claim was, 'Ali is the greatest', and to prove it, he would say, 'I am great and he will fall within eight' for his opponents. It was not a rhetoric, but was backed by solid practice and talent.

His boxing record was sensational, with 53 wins out of 55 fights – 35 out of those were knock outs! His most historical match was with Frazier in 1975, where they both fought tooth and nail, and MA finally won in the fifteenth round, when Frazier could not take the fight anymore. He was the king of the boxing ring for 27 long years, which required tremendous courage, utmost dedication, and of course, passion to be the number one in his field.

My toughest fight was with my first wife.

– Muhammad Ali

Moral of the Story of Muhammad Ali

• Sometimes one incident can change your whole life.

• With passion, you require hard work and focus for success.

• Only strong passion can make you fight for 27 long years. Nothing else can.

• In every game and profession, one should be innovative and develop one's own style. That style style should evolve around your strengths. In his case, it was powerful legs, stamina, and long reach.

He who is not courageous enough to take risks, will accomplish nothing in life.

– Muhammad Ali

EDWIN LAND

Passionate Scientist, and a Focused Inventor

This man who rose to be the CEO of Polaroid Corporation was passionate about the field of optics. He was an innovator, and came up with novel ideas which could transform pure science to applied technology. A very successful businessman, and an industrialist, he viewed himself more as a scientist than anything else.

Edwin Land's fascination with science began as a child. He was always playing with machines of his times, and would dismantle and reassemble anything he laid his hands on. He often used to be reprimanded for such actions, but this never discouraged him from experimenting. He would find his joy in the library, and read books on optics at bed time – such was his love for science in general, and optics in particular.

Land was captivated when, at the age of 13, his teacher demonstrated an experiment on how light polarising glass crystal can suppress the glare of light from a table top. To follow what he loved, he dropped out of Harvard, and started experimenting with polarisation. He was the one who used sheets of polarising plastics in front of the car headlights to eliminate the night time glare. He later set up a laboratory in Harvard, took loan from his father, and finally came up with a product which he could get a patent for. He called it Polaroid. He did his business with Eastman Kodak, by making camera filters. Polaroid was probably the most significant invention in the field of optics in the last century.

He was the one who developed the idea of 'instant photography'. This idea struck him when he was on a family holiday, and wished to view the photograph immediately. In just one year, he was ready to launch the camera, which would give you photograph instantly! They generated huge market for their new cameras, simply by word-of-mouth publicity. Polaroid cameras became synonymous with high technology in those days, and were amongst the world's most popular cameras.

Edwin Land also worked for the US government as an advisor, working to build the U-2 spy planes and spy satellites. His contribution of the 3D photography were very helpful to the American Defense, while his vectorgraphy technique was used to survey the French coast before the famous Normandy Landings, during the end of the Second World War. Although a scientist at heart, he was very quick to learn about the business side of technology. He wanted to put in efforts where he could build products for the masses at the right price. He was, of course, very creative, and understood that one had to fail a number of times before finally succeeding in life. In his lifetime, he received a total of 535 patents. He ran Polaroid for about 50 years, retired in 1980 as the CEO, but he continued experimenting and working in his field until his death.

Moral of the Story of Edwin Land

- Reading can be a source of inspiration and learning.

- Sometimes passion can be for a very specific field of interest. In this case, it was optics.

- An idea can get you fame, provided, you act upon that idea.

- One should learn how to develop one's passion into a marketable skill.

- A domain expertise must be clubbed with marketing and business skills, to maximise the impact of your enthusiasm on people.

Let us Recapitulate

• The highest common factors for success

Having read about the success stories of 10 people from domains ranging from art, music, adventure, sports, business, software, and science, one should be able to draw some conclusions. Each story gave us the strong points; passion and drive of an individual which made him or her achieve a larger-than-life status. But if we look at these lessons in totality, we should be able to make a list of things which forms the essence of it. In a way, these are the highest common factors for success.

- All successful people have passion for their work in sizeable proportion.

- Passion can kindle at any point in life.

- Reading in general, and in your specific domain of interests, is very essential to generate drive.

- Children must be encouraged to read.

- You must make a marketable product of your skills and drives.

- You must diversify and proliferate. Be prepared to take a little risk.

- An idea can win money and fame, only if you act upon it.

- Along with drive and enthusiasm, you require hard work and dedication for success.

- Strong passion gives you energy and determination to remain in your field of interest for a very long time – Possibly a lifetime.

- Most of the successful people slightly underestimate their own capabilities.

- You must develop your own style within your domain, and be different from others.

- Values and integrity is required for success in every walk of life.

- Curiosity could be the biggest gift of God.

- Inspiration can come from very small things.

- You must meet as many people as possible, because you learn from each one of them.

- Don't worry about what others think of you.

- Follow your drive, and money will follow you. Enjoy the journey.

> Three passions, simple, but overwhelmingly strong, have governed my life: the longing for love, the search for knowledge and, unbearable pity for the suffering of mankind.
>
> *– Bertrand Russel*

YOUR PERSONAL ROAD MAP

1. Read about three successful people from different fields or professions. For each one of them, list ten reasons for their success. Thereafter, tick those qualities that you feel you also possess. Note down those strengths which you need to develop. Shortlist three of those, and work on them for the next three months.

2. Write down five most important qualities that one must possess for success.

3. Rate yourself on the scale of 10 for the following.
    (a) Do you get inspired by small things?
    (b) Are you generally a curious person?

(c) Do you efforts to meet more people and make friends?

(d) How important is money to you?

(e) How much do you read in general?

(f) How much do you read in your domain?

(g) How much is your involvement in what you do?

(h) Do you take some risks in life?

(i) Do you have a strong desire to achieve any goal that you set for yourself?

(j) Do you believe in values and clean business dealings?

Now work on the areas where you have scored 5 points or less. Wherever you have scored more than 5 points, there is a reason to celebrate and take these as your solid strengths, which will help you succeed in life.

5

Creative Competence
Thinking out of the Juke Box

Creativity is the fragrance of individual freedom.

– Osho

PASSION AND CREATIVITY

There is a direct connection between passion and creativity. People who are creative in a particular field, are actually in love with their work, and are passionate about their work. Creative writers love writing, music composers love music, and painters are passionate about painting and art. In fact, if one has to be creative, then one must possess some degree of passion.

We, in this chapter, will look at creativity and innovation in a much larger perspective. For a day-to-day innovation at workplace, you have to have some degree of involvement, commitment, and passion for your work. Let us first look at what creativity is.

What is Creativity?

According to the dictionary, creativity means, 'To cause, to bring into, to come into existence, to portray for the first time'.

Simply put, it is the ability to create. Dictionary definition being too rigid, I would like to say that if you simply do something out of the ordinary, then it can qualify to be a creative activity. Creativity, therefore, is not limited to artists, scientists, composers, and poets alone. In the broader sense, we all are creative, and we all can be creative. We all demonstrate creativity on a daily basis. Even cooking an omelette in a different way is a creative activity.

How do you organise your wardrobe, how you arrange the pots and plants in your garden, how you set up your perfumes and aftershaves on the dressing table, and how you make a cocktail, could all be termed as creative activities. People are crazy about gardens, drawing room arrangements, and the way the food is prepared. They get involved in all these activities and display creativity and innovation. Therefore, there is a direct link between creativity, enthusiasm, innovation, and involvement. People who are passionate, are creative, and people who are creative are passionate about what they create.

Still larger Perspective

When you do something out of the ordinary – being creative – you are doing so many things at the same time. You are using your imagination, you are being original in your ideas, you are being bold, you are experimenting, you are being innovative, you are being flexible, you are also improvising, and to top it all, you are being adventurous! How about making an omelette? Creating the wackiest one would involve all that.

Managing a problem is creativity. In fact, all managers try to find solutions to problems most of the time. The guy who can find a solution not prescribed in a book, or taught at a business school, is innovative! If a person who is furious and abusive enters a room where three people are sitting, the following might happen. One person gets equally hyper, and starts shouting back; the other person gets very scared, and keeps quiet because he doesn't know what to do; and the third person in the room talks to this angry guy, listens to his problems, gives him a piece of advise, and satisfies him in such a way that the angry man cools down and leaves the room as a fully satisfied, happy person.

This is nothing but highest form of creativity. This manager created a situation and a solution to satisfy the angry young man! Creativity is much beyond knowledge. The way knowledge is applied is creativity. This way you are giving some meaning, and some tangible shape to knowledge. Creativity is, therefore, imagination and action. Imagination is more important than knowledge.

Creativity is the greatest rebellion in existence.

− Osho

If one has to be creative, one has to be different, and for that, you have to get rid of conditioning. Conformists can never be creative, because they stick to the beaten path, and that is why creativity is a form of rebellion. All those who are creative are courageous.

It is not E = mC²

In the larger sense, creativity doesn't mean something totally new. It is fine as long as it is different. A mother creates a child, and all her children are similar, but not same. All children have the same anatomy, but each one is different. Similarly, those who are creative, simply use their imagination beyond the knowledge which is a common knowledge − known to most of us.

We use the words 'Great thinkers' for Confucious, Socrates, and Aristotle. They were not doctorates of philosophy, or PhDs. They were the ones who thought out of the box and presented things differently. They were also very bold about expressing their philosophies without mincing their words – and that is why their words of wisdom are respected even today. Osho came out with a philosophy which was different from others, and he dared to say what others didn't, and had the courage to speak his mind out.

> What moves men of genius, or rather what inspires their work, is not new ideas, but their obession with the idea that, what has already been said is still not enough.
>
> *– Engene Delacroix*

Modification is also creativity, in fact, it is the first step to creativity. When you take up a new assignment and make positive changes to the organisation handed over to you by your predecessor, it is a great form of creativity. You are creating a new environment in the organisation. And those who bring about a positive change in the environment, love their work, and in a way, are passionate about their job.

Every Job can be Creative

You can be creative in almost every profession. When you do things differently, you prove it to others that you are better than them. Lawyers, managers, teachers, consultants, and trainers, can all use innovations in their day-to-day life. How can a taxi driver be innovative? It is such a routine work. Now see this.

A taxi driver in Mumbai used his ingenuity to get a roaring business. He used to place newspapers, the telephone directory, and magazines on the rear seat for the passengers. He also provided a mobile for local calls, a cigarette on the house, and soft drinks, chocolates, chips, and mineral water on payment. He provided the control panel for recorded music close to the passengers sitting in the rear seat. This taxi became so popular that he was booked on the phone for the whole day by someone or the other. This is thinking out of the box.

People also use innovative ideas to steal. Con men are very creative, in fact, the most creative. They can find a loophole in the security which the security people themselves are not aware of. This has been depicted in films like, *The Great Train Robbery*, *Aankhen* where three blind people are used for robbing a bank or even *Mission Impossible*. The thieves did something which nobody could think of. In the same sense, and not surprisingly, fudging accounts to fool the systems is known as *creative accounting*.

IQ, EQ, and Creativity

IQ is no measure of creativity. A person with an average IQ level can be highly creative. Creativity tilts more towards the domain of emotional intelligence, which deals with competencies like drive, determination, courage of conviction, flexibility, and even raw courage to some extent. It is the desire to do things in a different manner, and better than others, that fuels innovation. You don't have to be a topper in your school or a gold medalist in the engineering course, to be creative. If you make a habit of solving day-to-day problems differently, you will become a creative person. It will also be a step towards generating enthusiasm.

You must do the thing you think you cannot do.

– *Eleanor Roosevelt*

Some Wrong Notions about Creativity

It must be clear by now that creativity has much larger connotation than what we normally perceive it to be. There are, therefore, some wrong notions about it, that many of us have. I will now briefly talk about some of these.

• Originality is inborn

Many a times people say that, 'you either have it in you or you don't'. This is not true because each one of us has a streak of creativity. Some of us make an effort to be creative and some don't. A person who is gifted with the skills of painting is a gifted artist. We mix this up with being creative. When he applies this gift, only then he becomes creative. Not before that.

Gift is what you have, modifying and applying it is creativity.

• Creativity is Easy

It is not. You have to work towards being more creative. People like Isaac Newton came up with new ideas, because they kept on applying their minds to what came into their minds!

• Only Artists have it

It is not a prerogative of artists and scientists alone. I have earlier given examples of con men, taxi drivers, and housewives, who have been innovative.

• It has to be Totally Original

In its applied form, it doesn't have to be totally original. Originality is only one aspect of creativity. How different or how unusual is your idea or product from the run-of-the-mill stuff in the same domain, is the measure of innovation. How Picasso draws a horse with one stroke of a brush and how M F Hussain draws a horse, are two different aspects. They are horses all right, but yet different. Therefore, both are creative.

People qualify to be creative, if they can draw detailed maps or designs of something. For example, someone writing an epic on a grain of rice. People who produce large number of replicas are also creative. An artisan making earthen pots in hundreds is also creative. In addition, how many variations of a product can you make, also qualifies you to be creative. A rocking chair can be made in hundred different ways! Depends on your ingenuity.

• It has to be something like a product

Handling situations, handling your boss, and sometimes handling your wife can call for creativity. New ideas and concepts are the work of innovation and creativity. Therefore, it need not be only an Eiffel Tower or a Taj Mahal or a Mona Lisa.

• It is only Present in the Young People

I feel the older you get, the more experienced you are. You have experienced so many variations that you are able to use your experience to rake in creativity. In fact, age is no bar at all.

• Creative guys Dress up as Geeks

I find this very funny. I meet people from school of arts or mass communication dressed up in torn jeans, an earring in one ear, kurta, and a three day stubble, trying to 'look like' creative people! Your dressing up has nothing to do with being creative. Creative people don't dress like geeks, and people who dress up like geeks, are not creative.

• Creative People are Crazy

Now this is another fast one. You don't have to have that 'kink' in your head to be creative. If you have, is it a bonus? Creative people are little bold, do things differently, and don't bother about what others think of their ideas or ideologies. This way sometimes they give the impression to those who think in a straight line, that they are off their rocker. That's all.

It is easy to be brilliant if you are not bothered about being right.

– Denis Healey

Stumbling Blocks

Before we even look into the aspect of 'How to become more creative' – which you actually can, I would like to highlight some of our weaknesses which act as stumbling blocks. These are purely attitudinal, and can be overcome by effort and logic.

• What will Others Say?

We always worry about what others think about us. This is the biggest stumbling block. If you have to be different, then be different – don't join the herd. If you are a part of the herd, then you are not different than the herd. Simple. And it requires a bit of courage to defy the herd. Remember, a sheep out of the herd always feels very insecure, and that is why it sticks to the herd.

• Aiming for the Bull's Eye

If you experiment and be different, then you cannot always be right. Right? So don't be a victim of Zero Error Syndrome. Be prepared to go wrong. Get rid of the fear of failure because failure is a part of life, and part of the creative process.

When we look for perfection, we are unable to take any criticism, and we become egoists. If you want to be creative, you must be able to take criticism in your stride.

There was a great sculptor who could carve any statue to total perfection. Once a palmist told him that his days were numbered, and he would die very soon. The sculptor got scared, but found a unique way of avoiding death. He carved 11 statues which were exactly like him. When Yamaraj, the God of Death came to take him away, he got very confused. He could not make out who was the real sculptor, because of these perfectly similar statues. So he went back and told God that it was impossible to find out who the actual sculptor was.

God suggested a unique idea and asked him to try it out. This time Yamaraj went and stood amongst the 12 figures and looking at them, and said, 'I am surprised that even a great sculptor can make small mistakes while making statues.' The sculptor who was hiding as one of the statues got very wild and totally forgot that he was hiding from death, and came out in the open and asked, 'What mistake are you talking about? These are all perfect because I can never make a mistake'. Obviously, he got nabbed immediately by Yamaraj, and was taken away.

The moral of the story is that ego, and the feeling that 'I can make no mistake', can be very costly, and will always come in the way of creativity.

• Trying to be the Best

People who are perfectionists are always self-conscious of the outcome. They want everything to move in a straight line. Such an attitude leaves no room for trying something new, and forces you to take the beaten path. Obviously it kills creativity.

• Intellect – That Excess Baggage

People with too much intellect and knowledge, may well develop 'fixed ideas'. In fact, they carry too much excess baggage and can't see beyond their tutored intellect. Intellect is the faculty of reasoning, and is distinct from feeling. Creativity is closer to your heart than head. Therefore, feeling becomes more important than raw logic if you have to be different. Therefore, think from your heart rather than your head.

• Firm Belief

As we live in an environment, we get influenced by our parents, teachers, friends, and family. These experiences have a lasting effect, and some beliefs get deeply embedded into our heads and hearts. Sometimes it is very difficult to think outside these beliefs. Therefore, many a times these influences may act negatively and impede creativity.

Modification is Creativity

Remember 'eureka'; that famous experiences of Archimedes in the bath tub where he got a brainwave on which Archimedes principle was formed? Now creativity need not be a 'eureka' everytime. In fact, most forms of creativity come into being as a step-by-step modification to something that already exists. If fashion designers are creative, then all they are doing is cutting a skirt in different lengths, with different coloured cloth, with different slits and different belts, with different borders, and with different diameters! Also, skirts came into existence more than 2000 years ago.

All they are doing is altering the same old skirt! We had been seeing ceiling fans with three blades from our childhood. Now I see some fans with four blades. That is innovation. A young man in a toothpaste company suggested that if you increase the diameter of the tube head by a few millimetres, then the volume of toothpaste splashed on a toothbrush will become one and a half times more. Length of the toothbrush remaining the same, you end up using more toothpaste every day. This pushes up the sales by 30 per cent. Eureka! All that was done was to modify the orifice for the tube, and if this is not creativity then what is it?

> The difference between the right word and the almost right word is the difference between lightning and lightning bug.
>
> *– Mark Twain*

When You Get it Just Right

I had a boss who was a prolific writer. His drafting was perfect, and it was a treat to watch him while he wrote out his speeches or drafted official letters. I learnt a lot from him. He used to write very fast, and if he didn't get the right word in the middle of a sentence, he would leave that space blank, and move on. Sometimes after writing a full paragraph, he would return to that blank space, to plonk the right word! He used to say that as he wrote, he would recollect the right word at the appropriate time, and then he would fill in that blank. And that used to be the perfect word.

Just like you have pure sciences and applied sciences, this is an applied creativity. Creativity also could be applied and pure in nature, when you come up with something totally new. This is pure creativity, and when you use innovation and modification on a day-to-day basis, it is applied in nature.

> I rewrote the ending to *A Farewell to Arms*, the last page of it, 39 times before I was satisfied.
>
> – *Ernest Hemingway*

How to Become Creative?

As I said earlier, all of us are creative, and have that streak of creativity. All that you need is a tug to become creative. Applied creativity can be easily inculcated, but you have to start by applying – making efforts. Here are some practical tips.

• Explore the Child in You

Kids are inquisitive, they are not bothered about what others think of them, they are fearless, and they don't carry excess baggage. Most importantly, they are prepared to learn. Let the child in you come out in the open.

Explore and experiment. Shah Rukh Khan in many of his interviews has said that he still has that child in him. That is why, as an actor, he is prepared to experiment with different roles. Creative person always tries all the possibilities, he tries different ways, often even the wrong ones. If you always follow the right way to do a thing, then you will never be creative. The child in you doesn't carry that excess baggage, and doesn't know the right way! That is why creators fool around. Those who can put their pride and ego at stake repeatedly, can do things that nobody thinks are worth doing.

• Be a Dreamer

Man dreamt of flying, so he invented an airplane. He dreamt of crossing the oceans, so he invented ships; and when he wanted to move fast on the land, he invented the horse carts and cars.

Dreaming is an essential part of creativity. People who think are called day dreamers. Those who think a lot during the day, think of the same things again while sleeping. Musicians, poets, authors, and composers, are all dreamers. Leaders dream about victory, entrepreneurs dream about their business, and national leaders dream about making their country a great place to live. If you go back into the history, you would realise that those countries which had honest leadership, and leaders who had some sort of a dream for their country, did very well.

Today, most of the developing countries have leadership which has neither any dreams nor are they honest.

• Be Ready to Learn

Good actors learn from their directors, co-actors, and even the cameraman! They learn by watching performances of real good actors. Assimilating all this, they not only improve their style, but improvise, innovate, and become creative.

I know only one thing, that I know nothing.

– Socrates

To become creative, you have to keep your mind open. Observe what is happening around you, because inputs from the outside are as important as flashes from the inside. Boman Irani, a noted actor, when asked in an interview as to how he could play such diverse characters, replied, 'An actor has to be very observant. You observe the character very critically, and then portray those fine nuances'.

• Finding Good Things in the Ordinary

You don't have to write a great book or compose a mind-blowing musical piece or draw an out-of-the-world oil painting, to be creative. Life is made up of small things. Cooking, doing up your garden, and fixing up an electrical gadget in the kitchen, are all activities where you can show and practice your creativity. These small or little actions become meaningful, and can become the trigger for great creative work. All great epics started as mere gossip and discussions. Later they became epics and gospels. Creativity is an attitude.

• Get Involved

Having passion for something alone, cannot get you anywhere. Action along with enthusiasm can. Similarly, a creative idea will remain only in your head or heart, unless you make efforts to make it see the light of the day. Conversely, people who don't get involved (and many people don't like to involve) in what is happening around them can never feel passion for anything, and obviously are far, far away from creativity. You can be creative – provided you get involved. Thus, great actors, scientist, inventors, entrepreneurs, military strategists, poets, and singers were totally involved in whatever they wanted to create.

> Good judgement comes from experience, and experience comes from bad judgement.

> *– Anonymous*

Bring some Method to the Madness: Creative Process

From the time you get an idea in your mind to create something or a project comes your way to finally finishing off the job, could be a long drawn process. I hate to use the word process because processes can never be creative, and in fact, they kill creativity. Creative excellence is somewhat chaotic, but I would like to bring some method to this madness by looking at various stages of implementing a creative process, which can give a final shape to a creative idea.

• Research Analysis and Preparation

Great movies are not just a flash of idea. They may start with a simple idea, which gets into a concept stage, and tremendous amount of research goes into this concept before a director even begins. The same goes for writing a book, a worthwhile article, or designing a piece of architecture.

One has to see what work has already been done in that area by others. What material or books can be read on the subject. Are there any gaps where nobody has looked into? (This is most important). Can I do something which nobody did till now? and if yes, then obviously you create something new. This is the most important stage because it becomes the basis of the fact as to how creative your work actually will be.

This is also the time you can consult others, who are into similar work. Never hesitate to consult; remember to always be inquisitive like a child. Collect all the material that you can lay your hands on. Thereafter, discard the portions that are irrelevant, and keep only the useful stuff.

At this stage, you can analyse and also assess about the strengths and weaknesses. In fact a proper Strengths, Weaknesses, Opportunities and Threats (SWOT) analysis can be done to see how relevant, how effective, and how innovative your product will be.

• Explore and Experiment: Stretch a Little

Having got the basics in place, now is the time to experiment – say, fool around a little. While preparing a new dish, you collect all the ingredients and put them in a casserole – you may then add a few drops of lemon juice and while the stuff is still cooking, take a little of it and taste it. It doesn't taste right, so you add a bit of pepper. If it is still not right you add a dash of capsicum sauce, and you do this till you are satisfied.

Experimenting is the most important aspect of creativity. The more you go beyond the boundaries, the more original or different you will be from others. Don't hesitate going on a tangent. In fact, research and analysis can be done by anyone. Only the bold can experiment, and they are creative.

• Criticise and Improve

It is important to criticise your own work. This is important if you want to improve upon your work. It is also a part of the creative process because, innovation is not a big bang. It has to be tried and tested again and again.

Remember Thomas Edison failed 999 times before he could invent an electric bulb. It was the biggest creation of the last century. It lit the world literally. This is the time to think, rethink, and think again. You could go for brainstorming, and ask others about what has been done till now. Let others taste the dish, and say, 'I feel you got to brew it a little more, and add a bit of salt and a pinch of ajinomoto. Doing these two simple things will give your dish a different flavour all together'.

• Chewing the Cud

Having explored the options, experimenting with options and criticism of your work, helps you absorb your idea deep into your being. It becomes a part of your body and soul. If the first three steps are sincerely attempted, the idea would have been fully imbedded in your head and heart.

At this stage, it is time to detach yourself from work and look at it dispassionately as a 'third party'. In other words, its like chewing the cud – just sit over it for a while. It helps in the digestive process for animals, and in the realm of creativity, it lets you digest and absorb the entire concept.

• Listen to the Flashes

This actually overlaps with chewing the cud stage. These are the flashes of wisdom which can pop in at any point of time. It happens more often when your mind is totally free. This is the stage of 'letting it go' for a while. Background processing goes on, or your subconscious mind keeps working on the project all the time, and you may experience new ideas, new angles, and sometimes totally new solutions.

When you write a book, you sit with the book, you sleep with the book, and you breath the book. You got to be excited about what you are doing, so that it is with you all the time. Many people get ideas when they go for walks (It happened to Albert Einstein). People get it while listening to music or even before going to the bed, or even in the restroom!

Many a times you get an idea as you are tossing left and right on your bed when you are unable to sleep. It is good to keep a paper and pencil next to your bedside because you may never know when an idea pops up in your mind. Unless you note it down there and then, you may forget it by the time it is morning. Remember, all this is going to happen if you are totally involved in your work, and you are passionate about your idea or product.

'Ideas come to you when you look for ideas.' Westing House discovered the idea of the air brake when he casually read in a journal that compressed air power was being used by engineers for tunnel building. I am sure when Archimedes said 'eureka' while having bath, he was thinking about the impurity in the king's crown and not dreaming about McDonalds Mahaburger! He was constantly thinking about the problem which he was asked to solve, and that is how he hit upon the solution.

• Polishing and Fine Tuning

While you write an article or a book, you go through a number of drafts. It involves writing, rewriting, and more of rewriting. Initial stages were devoted to, 'Let the child in you come out', or 'Let go' or 'Go on a tangent'.

But once you have firmed up on the core stuff and the product is ready it's time for baking it a little more or putting that fine garnish, or adding that handful of pistachios on top of the pudding. This is also the time to fine tune and give a bit of manicure to the product, so that it can shine.

Creativity is basically motivational in nature.

– Robert Weisberg

Instant Creativity

It is great to see James Bond throw a fully glowing electric heater into a bath tub, instantly killing a KGB agent. This is instant creativity when you use something at hand to save your life. People also call it presence of mind. Those who can concoct a story (in fact telling a lie) at the spur of the moment, are also equally creative. Try out, its not that easy. Coming up with a solution when you are under pressure, and at the same time when there is very little time available to save the situation, requires a creative ability and nerves of steel.

Creative People

A lot of research has been done to find out if creative people have some common traits or characteristics. For instance, what would be common to Albert Einstein, Socrates, Aristotle, Pablo Picasso, W A Mozart, M F Hussain, Amitabh Bachchan, Leonardo Da Vinci, Blaise Pascal, Marconi, Louis Pasteur, Samuel Morse, Ludwig Beethoven, Thomas Moore, Swami Vivekanand, Mark Twain, Leo Tolstoy, Robin, Michelangelo, Michael Faraday, and Galileo Galili? Now this is a fairly long and varied list of people who demonstrated creativity in the field of science, spirituality, art, music, and so on.

These people did have some common thread in terms of their behavioural traits. It was not one trait but a combination of many qualities. The list of 16 traits of creative people is as under.

1. Enthusiastic

2. Independent

3. Self-confident

4. Enjoyed adventure

5. High-energy level

6. Variety of interests

7. Spontaneity

8. Curiosity

9. Childlike playful nature

10. Risk takers

11. Good sense of humour

12. Persistent

13. Internally motivated

14. Self-disciplined

15. Good learners

16. Passion

I feel, that out of these 16, the most important ones would be enjoying adventure, variety of interests, curiosity, passion, persistence,and internal motivation.

If you don't apply your mind, it is obvious that you will not get any output. Very simply, 'you have to think to think'. Therefore, curiosity, motivation and a large operative canvas (variety of interests) and an adventurous spirit, facilitate creative thinking and creative action. If one has to learn something from those who have been very creative, then the best will be that we inculcate those traits as our own habits.

> There are two ways of being creative. One can sing and dance, or one can create an environment in which singers and dancers flourish.
>
> *– Warren G Bennis*

On many occasions, one may not be able to find a new idea, but in the long run, the habit of pausing and putting in effort to find a new idea always pays.

Creativity in Organisations

As I said earlier, creativity is beyond knowledge. We proudly say that we are in the knowledge age without realising what it really means. Information available on the Internet is knowledge, books and CDs are knowledge as well.

If you see some of the many definitions of knowledge, you would realise that knowledge is repetitive, it is existent, to an extent, stagnant. It is a repository! Some of the definitions of knowledge are:

- 'Knowledge is the awareness and understanding of facts, truths, or information gained, in the form of experiences or learning or through introspection'.

- 'Knowledge is an appreciation of the possession of interconnected details which, in isolation, are of lesser values'.

- 'Arrange, define, duplicate, label, list, memorise, name, order, recognise, relate, recall, repeat, and reproduce'.

- 'The facts or principles relating to a particular subject or subject area'.

Now none of these four definitions talk of creating something different, unusual, out of the ordinary, new, innovative, inventive, original. Therefore, creativity adds to knowledge, and if you are in the knowledge business and you want to enhance your business, then creativity better be your business.

'Knowledge without creativity is stagnant'.

In fact, creativity, which is akin to coming up with something new, is the survival mantra for any industry today. You could be operating an airline, running a cellular mobile phone service, running a hospital, managing a hotel, manufacturing cars or computers, developing software, and this list could go on and on. You got to be different than others, and that is how you will be able to beat the competition. That is the difference between the old and the new economy. The old companies which did not change according to the times, and were not alert about newer concepts, had to shut shop.

To survive, you have to keep pace with the change but to excel you got to be creative. Earlier, the bigger would swallow the smaller, but today, it is the faster that will kill the slower. In the near future, the creative will beat the unimaginative. It is going to be creative capital and creative economy.

Creative Capital

Today, a company's most important asset is not the raw material, logistics, information networks, political clout, knowledge management, or even cash flow. The ball game has changed. It is going to be the creative capital. Just imagine Sabeer Bhatia, a young entrepreneur, making the US$400 million in a couple of years. It was an idea, it was creativity, and it was innovation as per the times. A good idea can get you venture capital, people to back you, people to work for you, and whatever else you need.

There is no dearth of money, provided you have an idea. This could look very lucrative for people like Sabeer Bhatia or somebody starting a business from a garage. Is it as much applicable to the giants who are sitting on billions of dollars and brand equity? Oh yes, it is very important for large corporations if they want to expand and do better than others. Creative employees create new products, new technology, new avenues, and new industries.

Most top jobs pay you for thinking, and not for running dat-to-day operations. I call it 'mental gymnastics'. Also, the CEOs who carry on with the day-to-day operations are doing somebody else's job! If this is the mindset of the people at the top level, then God help the guys down the line.

What I am trying to get to is that the top management must create a 'creativity culture', which allows people to think differently, come up with new and even bold ideas, and simply contribute to the bottom line.

Chaotic Nature of Creative Process

The latest jingo in the corporate world is that, 'our systems are in place'. I have heard this jargon, so many a times from the higher echelons, often beating their chest with pride, that I have developed an allergic response to the word 'systems'. Without naming any company, I would like to say that there are large corporations who have a complex bureaucratic process to buy even a pen – and they are proud of it! This in fact impedes efficiency, and definitely kills creativity. In the strict sense of business, systems, quality checks, and productivity, do take a very important place in terms of business imperatives. With such divergent requirements, how do you ensure creativity which is a chaotic process, to thrive while following systems, quality, and productivity. The concept of 'think tank' possibly started with the idea of letting a few people just do nothing else but thinking.

In fact in the US, there are many academicians who teach in the universities, and are taken into the national policymaking framework. Two things happen in such a case:

- First, the academicians are not under any pressure because of the nature of their jobs, and hence are free to air their views.

- Second, they actually are not responsible to implement the policy, and are not directly held responsible if something backfires.

In such a scenario, they take the full liberty to go even on a 'tangent', and make suggestions, which may otherwise seem outrageous for an official in the US Government to even utter.

This model worked very well for the policymaking exercise. In addition, it allowed the government to take a third party view on various subjects.

People like Henry Kissinger and Margaret Albright who shifted from an academic career to join the federal government, realised the difference between suggesting policy changes sitting in the university premises, and actually implementing them as secretary of state.

The main drawback of the think tank concept is that, it allows only a few people to think and suggest. This way you are losing out on the suggestions of a large number of people in the organisation. Start a thinking 'swimming pool' with everybody in it!

How to Encourage Collective Creativity in the Organisation?

Creating the collective creativity capital is the direct function of top leadership. Once the top management decides to invest in the creative capital, then the next step is to get it implemented up to the grass-root level, throughout the management hierarchy. Remember, creativity is an intangible asset, and greatly contributes towards the creative economy. Systems and processes directly contribute to the bottom line in terms of cash, which sometimes excites the top management so much, that they put creative capital on the back burner.

Taking the example of Symbiosis, which today is an internationally recognised education institute, one would observe that creativity has been one of the main pillars of its success. Dr S B Mujumdar, who is the founder of this wonderful organisation, believes in every institute to develop its own identity. The heads of the institutes numbering more than 30, are at total liberty to be innovative, inventive, and creative. Those heads of the organisations who further perpetuate this creative culture into the organisation, tend to leverage the benefit highly, because they allow collective creativity to flourish. Those who don't, they don't.

The same culture can also be implemented in a hard core business with a similar enthusiasm, provided there is a 'management will' in the organisation. Let me assure you that in organisations, there is a direct link between work environment and creativity. Business creativity is different than what Picasso and Mark Twain possessed. In case of a business environment, you need to come up with ideas that are workable, and yet different than the already existing run-of-the-mill ideas in the domain. For that, you need domain expertise, will (motivation), passion, and creative thinking to do it.

By and large every employee can think out-of-the-box, provided you let him do that. So, to a large extent, creative capital exists; the only thing is that managers and supervisors don't let the genie out of the box.

Managers concentrate only on developing the job skill-sets, and that is 'expertise' for them. They motivate you to learn, but do very little to motivate creative thinking, and let people be inspired to do something different.

Managers can positively influence and induce all the four aspects of creativity, i.e., expertise, intrinsic motivation, enthusiasm, and skill to think creatively. As far as motivation for the purpose of creativity is concerned, the intrinsic motivation is far more effective than the extrinsic one. Extrinsic motivational factors are those which come from outside like promotions, awards, pay hikes, etc. They motivate people to work hard, but are not necessarily useful for generating or encouraging creativity. Stimulation, enthusiasm, and intrinsic motivation are more environment related, and managers and the organisational culture should work towards the following:

1. Freedom to work and discuss

2. Providing challenges

3. Providing resources

4. Managerial encouragement

5. Organisational support

6. Avoiding Zero Error Syndrome

In large organisations, collective creativity is not killed by one or two managers. It is collectively killing collective creativity what is widespread in the entire environment. Many people are afraid of even challenging it. That is why it is the duty of the top management. Some organisations go a step forward, and even involve their customers in the collective creativity process. You are making the customers so passionate about the product that he or she will also actively give you creative inputs about the product.

DO'S AND DON'T'S
Do's

- Encourage people to speak up.

- Encourage people to experiment.

- Clear petty obstacles.

- Reduce democratic rigour as far as possible.

- Ask people to write white papers, read books, and provide them with tools to update knowledge.

- Appreciate for achieving results, and also 'attempting' to create new things.

- Encourage even small innovations, which may be insignificant.

- Help workers feel good about what they do.

Dont's

- Do not have time-consuming layers of evaluation. This puts people off from coming up with an idea again.

- Do not create fear of Zero Error Syndrome.

- Do not criticise people when they come up with new ideas.

- Do not place capable people in the wrong place. Managers often do this.

Creativity can benefit just any and every business. Even for a mundane job like accounting, where people thought there can be no innovation, 'activity-based costing'–which is a recent innovation – is a new business revolution.

Parting Shot

Keeping a balance between creativity and systems, as well as operational discipline, is a difficult task for any organisation. SAS? as an organisation has been able to manage creativity in the organisation by following the simple principles of rewarding excellence and innovation, minimising bureaucratic tangles, providing on-the-job challenges, and updating their tools.

Let us Recapitulate

- Passion and Creativity

  There is a direct relation between passion and creativity. Those who are creative in a particular field are in love with their work.

- What is Creativity?

  Creativity is the ability to create something out of the ordinary. We can be creative on a day-to-day basis. Therefore, creativity is not limited to fine arts alone.

- Still lasrger perspective

  Handling people, managing a situation, and managing a bad boss are all creative activities. It is imagination and action.

- It is not, something totally new

  Anything can be creative as long as it is different. It doesn't have to be totally new.

- Every job can be creative

  Every profession allows you to be creative. Lawyers, managers, teachers, and trainers can be creative on a day-to-day basis.

- IQ, EQ, and creativity

  IQ is no measure of creativity. EQ does have a correlation with doing something different. It is the desire to do something different than others, that fuels innovation. This desire falls under the Emotional Intelligence domain.

- Some wrong notions about creativity
    ◊ Originality is inborn
    ◊ Creativity is easy
    ◊ Only artists have it
    ◊ It has to be totally different and original
    ◊ It has to be something like a product
    ◊ It is only present in the young people
    ◊ Creative guys dress up as geeks
    ◊ Creative people are crazy

- Stumbling blocks
    ◊ What will others say?
    ◊ Aiming for the bull's eye
    ◊ Trying to be the best
    ◊ Intellect is an excess baggage
    ◊ Firm belief

- Modification is creativity

- When you get it just right

- How to become creative
    ◊ Explore the child in you
    ◊ Be a dreamer
    ◊ Be ready to learn
    ◊ Finding good things in the ordinary
    ◊ Get involved

- Bring some method to the madness: creative process. Creative creation can be a long process. Try to make this process a little structured. Some steps could be as follows:
    ◊ Research analysis and preparation
    ◊ Explore and experiment
    ◊ Criticise and improve^Chewing the cud
    ◊ Listen to the flashes
    ◊ Polishing and fine tuning

- Instant creativity

    Acting on the spur of the moment to do something new

- Creative people

    People who are creative have certain traits like, enjoying adventure, passion, curiosity, etc.

- Creativity in organisations

    To survive, you have to keep pace, but to excel, you got to be creative. It is especially important in the knowledge-based society, because creativity adds to knowledge.

- Creative capital

    The most important asset of the corporate world is creative people.

- Chaotic nature of creative process

  Too much and too rigid a process can kill creativity.

- How to encourage collective creativity in the organisation

  Top management must encourage everybody to contribute to the creative effort.

- Parting shot

  It is important to keep a balance between creativity and systems that run the organisation.

Your Personal Road Map

1. List 10 professions and justify how each one of them can be a creative profession. (Use your creativity)

2. If you look at four aspects of creativity listed under, then mark which ones are your strengths, and which are your weaknesses. What efforts can you make to strengthen your weak points?
   (a) Originality
   (b) Ability to produce in large quantities
   (c) Flexibility: Producing different versions of the same thing.
   (d) Ability to elaborate and going into great details (for example drawing a complex blueprint or intricate artwork).

3. List your fears that block creativity.

4. Look at your resume. Does it show your creative side? If not, add at least three of your creative skills in your CV. For example, a prolific speaker, enthusiastic amateur writer, etc.

5. Observe your daily chores. How enthusiastic are you in terms of originality? For the next one week, try at least one unusual thing a day and surprise others.

6. On the scale of 10, mark yourself on the following traits:
    (a) Curious
    (b) Ad
    (c) Risk taker
    (d) Enthusiastic
    (e) Energy level
    (f) Varied interests
    (g) Persistent
    (h) Self-disciplined
    (i) Good learner
    (j) Can go against criticism
    (k) Defiant
    (k) Playful in nature

    There are one dozen basic traits listed here, which are very important for you to be creative. Your scores will indicate your weak areas or traits that need to be improved upon. You will have to make a sincere effort to improve upon those areas where you score less than six. For example, you cannot attempt to be creative, unless you are a bit defiant and can go against criticism. If you score less than six on any of these points, then accept them as your weakness, and make a sincere effort to bring about a change.

7. What three things do you want to change in your organisation, so that people (your peers and subordinates) can become more creative?

    The most crucial factor in creativity is the motivation to do something creative.

    — Teresa Amabile

6

Arousing Enthusiasm in Your Organisation

Passion Capital

Enthusiasm is the greatest asset in the world; it beats money, power, and influence.

— Henry Chester

INDIVIDUAL VERSUS TEAMWORK

In the last few chapters, we examined passion as a trait at an individual level. Majority of us work in organised groups called organisations, corporations, or teams. It is important to be energetic and involved individually, so that you can be successful. It is equally important for you to select like-minded committed people for your organisation or your team, so that they together perform better than other organisations in the same business. It is also a duty of each person to arouse inspiration in his teammates, and also in the entire organisation that he or she works for. Each one of us contributes towards the passion capital of the organisation, and helps to raise the PQ of the entire lot.

The Three Entities

When you want to arouse passion into your people then you have to look at the people, the environment, and yourself. Remember you create an environment, and you are responsible for your own conduct. Right from a junior executive to the CEO, we all contribute to either create, or crush the work environment. Therefore, environment becomes the collective responsibility of all the people in the organisation.

Everyone of us has a sphere of influence. Some of us directly influence only five people, and some may influence the worklife of hundreds of people in the organisation with their personal conduct. It is, therefore, very important to understand the affect of ones own behaviour on the people around. You can either positively influence people, so that their morale remains high, and they are passionate about what they do at workplace, or you may negatively influence and kill their enthusiasm.

Remember, 'People don't quit jobs, they quit bosses'. So getting enthusiastic people on board is one problem, and to let them remain enthusiastic and arouse passion in those who are not, is another. Both of these are leadership functions. Let us look at the people in the organisation first.

> You can have the most beautiful dream in the world, but it takes people to build it.
>
> *— Walt Disney*

Passionate People on Board

All other things equal, a vibrant person is a prized possession of an organisation. It is the biggest tangible and intangible asset. It is intangible, because it is not straight away visible when you hire a person, and it is tangible because it has a profound effect on the performance of the individual, his co-workers, and the organisation as a whole, and goes beyond the organisational boundaries as well; as we shall see very soon.

Such people perform better, because they love to perform. They put their heart and soul into their jobs, and their attitude is infectious, which goes on to motivate and charge up the whole team. They are natural high performers, often going beyond the call of the duty, and their output can far exceed their less passionate co-workers. They also have higher commitment to the organisation, and derive more job satisfaction than others.

There are people who are natural enthusiasts, or are generally inspired by lots of things – in other words, almost everything. These perpetually motivated people take interest in every activity that you can think of.

Obviously, with such high general PQ, these people will also be demonstrating affinity for their work. This may not be true in all cases. Therefore, besides overall enthusiasm levels, we need to look at the components that are responsible for generating enthusiasm for the work that people do. We will look at some of these aspects as we proceed.

Larger Role of an Employee

It is not only important for an employee to do his job well and do it with enthusiasm, but it is equally important for him to influence others around him positively. Such a person can add a lot of value to an organisation.

• Impact on the Job

The creation of nature, i.e. man, is an optimum unification of body, mind, and soul. Any employee who is passionate, has all three aspects fully synchronised, and obviously he will out-perform others. Such people have a sense of pride, confidence, and self-worth. They are less fearful of losing their job, and are more truthful in their expression and opinions.

• Impact on Internal Environment

Passion is contagious. A good enthusiastic employee has a very positive influence on his team, and indirectly sets an example for many. Such people act as great motivators for the organisation as a whole. They make the workplace more challenging and exciting. They are also prepared to innovate and experiment.

• Impact on the External Environment

Today, word-of-mouth publicity can really make or mar a business. If a nurse goes and tells her friends about unhygienic conditions of the pathological labs and operation theatres in the hospital she works for, imagine the negative impact it will have on the hospital. Alternately, imagine the positive impact if another nurse who works for a good hospital goes and praises her workplace to be the cleanest and the best.

In today's economy, workers have a large radius of influence – much larger than their 5 ft by 5 ft workplace. They can influence the mindset and perception of the customers in a positive or a negative manner. They can also add to the customer base even if they are not in the marketing department, because each employee, regardless of his/her job profile has a direct contact with many people.

In some cases they can make customers act as a marketing force, because they are impressed with the organisation. In short, every employee is your brand ambassador. When the alumnus of a good college goes to the industry, he becomes the brand ambassador of the college where he studied. It helps students of the next batches get better jobs because the industry has experienced good work before.

• Other Benefits

◊ Passionate employees work for the organisation because they love the job. If the environment is also good, then it is a great advantage. In such a case, people don't quit jobs easily even if they are offered more money by the competitors.

◊ They inspire loyalty in other co-workers.

◊ They have the courage of conviction as they are confident about doing their jobs well. Therefore, they would come up with honest inputs and suggestions so that the decisions are made on fact and not fiction.

◊ They influence positively towards team building.

◊ They are always ready to go that extra mile.

◊ They believe in the organisation and their product. When a workforce goes out to sell a product without conviction, then the success rate will be much lesser. For example, if a workforce is selling a book and each sales person has been briefed about the content of the book, then it becomes lot easier for him to convey this in a very convincing manner to the owners of bookstalls. Similarly, a lady who sells beauty products will market it effectively if she has used the products herself, and has been satisfied with its quality and result.

◊ Passionate employees are confident about their work and their abilities. They are also aware of their impact on the other people at workplace. Because of this, they are more often than not truthful in expressing their views. Such workers are unlikely to be sycophants, who agree with bosses just to please them. In today's competitive world, you require correct inputs to make business decisions, and the least you can expect is that your employees or teammates tell you the truth.

What a person tells you may not be pleasant or even palatable, but that information would be vital for the good of your business.

Every organisation in the world would like to have these dynamics that I have briefly portrayed above, at their workplace. But there are very few who have been able to achieve all these.

Getting the Right People

Getting the right people for an organisation is the most challenging job for the top management. What do we really mean by the right person? Is it only the skills or it is something more? Today, everybody knows that skills alone will not be able to see you through. We have to look broadly for a good positive attitude along with skills. In addition to a positive outlook, the most important emotional trait that a person must possess to perform is – *Passion for the Job*.

We have talked about passion as an affinity for something or some activity till now. We have also examined the general passion quotient, which broadly means how enthusiastic a person is in the overall sense. It is good to have high energy, and highly enthusiastic people on board, but will it serve the purpose in totality?

The answer is NO. As far as an organisation and a job is concerned, it is important to have people who are upbeat about the job, about the cause, and about the organisation they work for – in this order – a high general PQ is of course a bonus. Have you seen people joining a movement? They do it because they are convinced about the cause. A cause can convince you if it matches with your own set of values. When you see a purpose, your passion kindles. Sometimes it is sheer love for that activity. People who love mountain climbing make many attempts to conquer a peak. They are not dettered by frostbite, chilblains, or even pulmonary edema! These mountaineers take all this risk because they love to climb mountains. If you take a person who is highly enthusiastic in general for mountain climbing, he may agree to go once, but may not attempt repeatedly to conquer a peak in the face of death. Passion for the work that you do, therefore, is the most important factor for job satisfaction and productivity. People who love their jobs will always out-perform others. Such employees or teammates always have an impact on any business, which is far greater than it can be measured.

The company that you work for also matters. It is not only a great high-flying name that matters to you, but it is also important what that company stands for, or how the company is perceived by others, and its company profile. When you say IBM, or Tata, a bell rings in your mind. These companies have a very high credibility in the market, and anyone would be proud to associate themselves with such organisations. Once you join the organisation, the work culture or 'environment' also matters greatly.

People work for organisations who treat their employees well, despite lesser remunerations. Besides the organisation, it boils down to two things:

• Values

• Work preference and affinity for that work

In one of my interviews with the press, I was asked, 'What do you think success is?'

My answer was straight forward and I said 'Getting paid for what you love to do is success'.

Pilots, comedians, anchors, golfers, marketing guys, trainers, and professional speakers, all get a kick, a high out of what they do. If a surgeon loves being in the OT, feels good and involved while carrying out an operation, and is paid handsomely, he is surely successful. But if he can't look at blood, can't stand the smell of anesthesia, then the surgery is not his cup of tea. He may stick around because of the high compensation, but, would not truly be successful.

Selection Process

How do you select the right person with a high PQ? Many a times very little effort is made to look for adequate passion in a candidate for a job during the selection process. If interview panels are briefed about this aspect, then I feel it would make them apply their minds to look for this trait in every candidate they meet. There is no single test that can indicate the PQ of an individual, but a series of efforts by the interviewing panels can help make a serious assessment. Briefly, the following must be done:

- Behavioural interviewing
- Psychometric assessment of work preferences and values
- Detailed review about the previous job profiles
- Scrutinising the values that a person stands for
- Major achievement can be a great indicator of what the person likes
- Sometimes CVs do reveal the enthusiasm of a person
- Gut feeling of the experienced panel can be very handy

How the person has spent his spare time is also an indicator of likes and dislikes. During interviews for selecting people for business schools, I have realised that examining the fact as to how a person has spent his spare time is indicative of his drive. For example, if a candidate finished his engineering a year ago, and took one year's time for preparing for his entrance exam and his interviews, it is worth finding out if he did anything else other than preparing for the exam alone. There are people who, in addition to preparing for the competitive examination, study a foreign language, or enrol themselves in a short-term course on accounting and finance, or say a crash course on quality management. This indicates that a person's general enthusiasm level is high and can also give some idea about his/her job preferences.

It is yet not very clear how values and work preferences interact, because they are two different things. But in any case, both of them are important from the employees performance point of view. Sometimes, even a seasoned panel of interviewers may get carried away by a false mask or an outward positive appearance.

The following must be noted.

• A person who speaks with passion and enthusiasm, may not be actually enthusiastic about the job that he/she is seeking.

• One has to be beware of great actors who can well rehearse and pretend to be in love with the job.

• Outward exuberance and good presentation may be misleading.

Enthusiasm is contagious, you can start an epidemic.

– Anonymous

Creating the Right Environment

Having discussed the passionate person that you are looking for, its time to look at the organisational atmospherics and the people who create this environment, so that necessary bounce can thrive. So first let's look at those aspects which any employee would look for at his job place.

• Win–Win Situation

Every person who joins an organisation and works for it, must be convinced that there is something good for him. Therefore, the employee must see a win-win situation. If the organisation gains from him, then he should also gain something from the organisation. Therefore, it is important to see his viewpoint to ensure that his interest is always taken care of.

• Right Person for the Right Job

Most passionate people would lose their sheen when you put them into the wrong job. Therefore, don't try to fit a round peg into a square hole! This is the biggest damage that you can do to an individual as well as the organisation. Remember you took him onboard mainly because of the love that he has for the job. So now it's time to ensure that he remains in love.

We had a brilliant student who got a great job with a multinational company during the campus interview. In fact, she got the best company and the best salary package. She came to tell me that she was not happy with this! I asked her for the reasons for this dissatisfaction, and she told me that she had specialised in systems but was offered a marketing profile by the recruiters. I had a word with the team which had come for the interview about her apprehension. They told me that they would let her work in the marketing department for a while and observe her work preferences. Based on her inclination and performance they would consider placing her in the appropriate job profile; and six months later they did!

• Self–Actualisation

Remember, Passionate people work for the love of it. They always reach out to attain the state of 'self-actualisation' and seek 'self-worth'. Dr Abraham Maslow coined this term, which is the pinnacle within the hierarchy of human needs. He summed it up very well as, 'A musician must make music, an artist must paint, a poet must write, if he has to be at peace with himself'. Thus, what a man can be, he must be. If you don't let people do what job they want to do, then you are creating a mismatch.

• Freedom and Space

We all need our freedom and space. As long as one works within the framework of defined rules, or there is no clash of interests between the individual and the organisation, it is a healthy situation. Whatever be the job and whatever be the level of the employee in the organisational hierarchy, freedom and space is required for optimum performance.

• Purpose

Close on the heels of self-actualisation is the sense of purpose. If a person is working in the field of education, he should be made to feel that it is a noble and an honourable work. It is also a contribution to the society, and you can look at it even as a charity. In a country like India, people in the corporate jobs are paid much more than those who are into teaching – so it is an act of charity. You can also find a purpose and a dash of benevolence, because every year, hundreds of boys and girls find a job from your campus. If you want to generate enthusiasm, and motivate people, then there can be nothing better than showing people purpose in what they do. People seek purpose as per their own perception.

> Nothing is really work, unless you would rather be doing something else.
>
> *– James Matthew Barrie*

Perceptions and Values

People perceive things differently. One situation can be perceived and interpreted by three people in three different ways. This happens because people come from different backgrounds, different cultures, and different organisations. Due to this, they develop individual systems of values. These are so hardwired into individuals, that it is very difficult to change these value systems. The smartest way to handle people is to understand their value systems and communicate with them at that wavelength. It is like a radio network, where you transmit the frequency of the receiver.

If you want to communicate to a different receiver, then you change your frequency to match that of the new receiver. People develop values as a group, and rarely as individuals. For example, if you look at the Britishers, they are very stringent about punctuality. So when you interact with them, then make sure that you are absolutely punctual for all the meetings. If you are dealing with the Japanese, you can stress on trust. They usually believe in short-term contracts, and work on faith, honour, and trust. Americans will go into too much of systems approach, long-drawn contracts, and employ a very synthetic approach while interacting with people. In the Gulf region, it is again faith and honour and more often than not, they would honour their word.

What we learn with pleasure, we never forget.

– Anonymous

Convincing people simply means understanding their value systems. Great moviemakers who have been successful, have made movies of their times. They made what was acceptable to people at that point of time. In the sixties, it was the love stories that swept the Indian cinema. The seventies saw the rise of the rebel and the birth of the angry young man.

Movies didn't change the masses, but the masses changed the movies! In the international arena, the fifties and the sixties saw immense success of war movies, because the period was immediately after the World War II. Today you have science fiction movies, because the technology has changed, and so has the perception of people. To influence people, you got to understand what values they stand for.

Dr Groves came up with a model of values. According to him, societies, cultures, and even individuals, go through an evolution of values. This is how people belonging to these groups perceive the world, situations, and their jobs, and even their own worth. Over thousands of years of human civilisation, these need-based traits got developed in human beings. As the society developed, these eventually became values of the society. Different people got influenced by different sets of values. If you can understand the value system of an individual and deal with him accordingly, you can surely deal with him appropriately. This would also be the best way to arouse enthusiasm into your people.

I will briefly touch upon five values which matter in today's context.

• Tribal

A tribe was one of earliest forms of alliance. People came together to form tribes, which provided protection. The strongest became the chief, and people were prepared to give their lives for the chief. No questions were ever asked, as the chief was always considered correct. This got into the DNA as subservience, psycophancy, and sacrifice for the leader and hero worship. That is why even today we are sometimes surprised to see so much of subservience in the society.

• Rebellion and Might

This value system means survival of the fittest. Here, the strong dominates the weak. New challenges the old, and there is some kind of rebellion. This was the mentality of 'might is right' and soon it was realised that a more organised value system was required, which meant, systems, law and order, as well as stability.

• Law and Order

Obedience, discipline, and frameworks emerged, and rebellion, aggression, and chaos disappeared. The system and society provide security, authority, and order. To do well, you follow the system. This also brought about rigid thinking, cults, faith, and religions. Also, 'isms' like Marxism, terrorism, and so on, emerged. This became so overbearing over a period of time that people wanted to break away from these man-defined boundaries. Also, there was a move to become individually successful, powerful, and to seek rewards.

• Sense of Achievement

This is a materialistic value stage. Just achieve it, whatever be the price. People want to achieve at an individual level, and become a system themselves. Look at entrepreneurs like Bill Gates, Laxmi Narain Mittal, and Swaraj Paul. They were all driven by achievement. Most of the millionaires get a high because they are millionaires, and not because they spend millions! The sense of a big bank balance, huge real estate, and stocks, gives a sense of power and achievement.

• For the Society or for a Cause

This value comes into play when people want to turn inwards, and look inwards, and this is a phase of introspection and self-actualisation. You want to do it because you want to do it, and that's it. This is the time when people want to give it back to the system and the society. Sense of delivering, doing good, and contribution sets in.

> Would you tell me please, which way I ought to go from here, asked Alice in wonderland. 'That depends on where you want to go', said the Cheshire Cat.
>
> *– Alice in Wonderland*

While dealing with a person in the organisation, try to see what type of person he or she is. Most people would by and large fit into one of these five value systems. Thereafter, deal with them accordingly. You will be surprised at your success rate. In certain parts of our country, film stars are treated as gods. People construct temples and worship them. There are instances of uproars on their deaths – a strong demonstration of tribal mentality. Film stars surely win political battles in such regions. This is a mentality of 'hero worship'. There is also a streak of being 'awe struck'. This is mass psyche. People always need a strong visible leader. If you can provide anything close to this, you are sure to get loyalty.

There are film directors or producers who want to give back to the society by making films with a strong social message. As a story writer, there is no point of writing a murder mystery for such directors; they will never accept it. So understand what a person wants and then design your approach to handle or sell and idea to him/her accordingly.

An Environment that Inspires

> To live is to choose, but to choose, you must know who you are and what you stand for, where you want to go, and why you want to get there ....
>
> *– Kofi Annan*

If we analyse what has been said by Kofi Annan, whole lot of clarity will dawn upon us regarding the business that we do. In the corporate world, our value statements and missions, spell out who we are and what we stand for. Vision gives us where we want to go – the destination. Corporate strategy is there to tell us the 'how' to get there to your destination. What about the why? The 'why' in most of the cases is missing! The reason why you exist, you do business, or what you do, is Passion. If you can convince the people that the job is worth doing, then passion automatically kindles. Once the 'why' is clear, it is important to light the inspiration. Here are a few things that should be looked into:

• Challenge and Excitement

If you want people to work with enthusiasm, then the first thing that needs to be done is getting excitement and challenge into the work. This component of human behaviour can never be compensated or triggered by monetary rewards. It is easier said than done, and requires all the skills and charm of leadership and creativity to get your team excited about what they do on the day-to-day basis. Even if you can remove the mundane, routine, drudgery of work, by 10 per cent, you have made a beginning.

• Allow Experimenting and get People Involved

Have you seen a bunch of kids playing on a beach, making houses, roads, tracks, tunnels, and imaginary townships, castles, bridges, palaces, and airport with mere sand – they make what they can imagine. Sand allows them to shape their imagination. During the Great Depression of America, the then president of the US saw a bunch of kids making townships and roads with sand, which gave him an idea of building a nation. His idea was simple – If one dozen kids can remain engrossed making roads and buildings for hours in the sand then why don't we involve the entire unemployed workforce to build skyscrapers and roads. This strategy helped in building an entire nation.

Every person has a child in him. Wake up that child in your people, and that is a function of leadership. Get people involved, and let them experiment, so that passion thrives in your organisation.

• Empower the Organisation

Good film directors explain the context and the scene in detail to the actor before a shot. Good directors leave it at that, and allow the actor to deliver the dialogues and enact according to his or her abilities. Good actors understand the need of the director and interpret the scene accordingly, and then deliver with full gusto. This is empowered inspiration. In organisations, leaders are the directors, and people in their teams are actors. People must be clear about their jobs, must be allowed freedom to execute and deliver as per their abilities and choices. A little autonomy goes a long way to generate enthusiasm. Many organisations fail to deliver because there is too much control.

• Minimise Criticism

For passion to thrive, you need to minimise criticism. How can you expect a person to invest his heart into his work when he is often being criticised? This doesn't mean false praise or the likes. All I am saying is to keep a check on criticism, and resort to it if there is no other way out.

• Let People See Reason

A nine-year old boy used to suck his thumb, and kept on happily sucking it, despite threats and scolds by his parents. They took him to a child specialist. The child specialist followed a simple approach. He told this young boy that it was absolutely fine for a boy his age to suck his thumb, because a nine year old is too young. The boy was quite pleased, because nobody had told him that before. Then the doctor said that it is when you reach a double digit age of 10 years that you stop sucking the thumb! Having said this, he sent the boy back home with his parents. This boy kept sucking the thumb thereafter, and surprisingly, just one month before his tenth birthday he stopped it completely!

You have to make people see reason so that they get convinced. It is often easy to convey, but difficult to convince. Once convinced, people put in hard work, and even change their negative attitudes (thumb sucking) which are more or less a habit with many of them.

• Walk the Talk

In battlefields, the leaders have to be in front. They walk the talk. Leading by example is the best way to infuse enthusiasm. Good leadership means doing what you preach. Once people see responsible people walking the talk, they start walking themselves.

Matching the Man with the Organisation

Having created a good organisational atmospherics, you should keep innovating so that people always remain aligned to the vision and goals of the organisation they work for. Some simple tips are:

• Discussions

Let people discuss their work, their success, achievements, and even failures. This is the best way to communicate with people.

• Feedback

Take feedback from people. What do they feel about the work they are doing? Is there a mismatch between what they want and what they actually do? If there is, then you must take corrective measures to ensure they find meaning in what they do.

• Let People Express Their Opinions

This is a tough nut to crack. This can happen only if this is drafted into the organisational culture at all levels. People feel claustrophobic if they are not allowed to speak their minds and hearts. One must remember that encouraging people to speak up, not only makes them feel empowered and a part of the organisation, but also gives the top management certain inputs which were not otherwise thought of.

• Don't Kill the Spirit

It is very difficult to nurture passion, it may perhaps take years to build vibrant organisations, but it takes very little time to suppress enthusiasm. Some of these spirit killers for your team are listed as under:

- Many a times people are asked to tell lies to customers or clients.
- No credit for being innovative is given.
- People are asked to do things which are contrary to the organisational values, which are often put in writing.
- People are not fully trusted.
- Politics is allowed to breed in the organisation.
- Favouritism is shown for some by the bosses.
- People are put down or ticked off in front of others.

Try to see which out of these are problem areas in your organisation, and then try and take corrective actions.

Let us Recapitulate

- Individual versus Teamwork

- The three entities

  People, the environment, and you – All these three are important to make creativity happen.

- Passionate people onboard

  Vibrant people are a prized possession. They are the biggest asset of an organisation.

- Larger role of employees

  Every employee must add value to the organisation. The value addition can be in terms of impact on the internal as well as external environment.

- Getting the right people

  Over and above the skill-sets, an employee must possess passion for the job.

- Selection process

  Series of efforts by an experienced interviewing panel can help in locating people who have passion for that particular job.

- Creating the right environment

  Every employee who wants to contribute to the organisation looks for the right work environment. The organisation should provide the following:
  - ◊ Win-win situation
  - ◊ Right person

◊ Self-actualisation

◊ Freedom and space

◊ Purpose

- Perceptions and Values

  Convincing people means understanding their value systems. The management must deal with people according to their individual perceptions to get the best out of them.

- An environment that inspires

- Matching the man with the organisation

YOUR PERSONAL ROAD MAP

1. Critically evaluate your organisation and answer the following questions:

   (a) Does your organisation make an effort to find out if a person is passionate about the job he or she is seeking? If the answer is no, then list out steps that can be taken to incorporate this in your human resource policy.

   (b) Does your top management look at an employee as a brand ambassador of the company or merely as an employee?

   (c) Does your organisation practice what it gives out as its values and ethics?

2. Do you allow people in your team to experiment? Do you allow them to make mistakes?

3. Make a conscious effort to understand five of your immediate subordinates, and try to map them into five values described in this chapter. Thereafter, make it a habit to deal with each one accordingly. Observe the difference it makes.

4. Conduct the following activities for your team once every fortnight, for an hour.

(a) Have a one-on-one feedback session with each person of your team.

(b) Have an open discussion, wherein you should take in suggestions regarding how the work goes on in your department.

(c) Encourage people to express their opinions.

5. Make a habit of observing your team, and identify the special abilities that each one has. If the job permits, try to relocate people into job profiles which best suit their abilities.

Life is either a daring adventure, or nothing. Security does not exist in nature, nor do the children of men, as a whole, experience it. Avoiding danger is no safer in the long run than exposure.

– Helen Keller

7

Passion at Schools and Colleges
Lighting those Small Candles

It will be possible to describe everything scientifically. But it would make no sense. It would be without meaning. As if you described a Beethoven symphony as a variation of wave pressures.

– Albert Einstein

OUR EDUCATION SYSTEM

There are numerous debates about how good or how bad our education system is, and most of the time in these intellectual discussions, the education system is always in the firing line. It is a favourite subject for researches, discussions, and white papers, which always are more than happy to point a finger at every and any education system.

Yes, there can always be room for improvement, but you cannot discard or ridicule a time-tested system, which has been existing for such a long time. With this very education system, we as a society have progressed very well till now, and have been able to come up with great inventions and discoveries, which have made a very positive difference to our quality of life in all respects. In the last hundred years, our standard of living has improved manifold. Great musicians, film actors, poets, artists, lawyers, doctors, engineers, and pilots are the products of the same system.

If all this has been achieved, then it will be unfair to criticise the existing education system so blatantly, as we often do. Let us also get one thing clear that it is not necessary that everything new or modern has to be good or has to be right. The education system in its present form is pretty okay, because it has served its purpose to a large extent. Different people have defined the purpose of education differently. I feel the definition by Martin Luther King Jr. is simple, precise, and to the point, which says, 'Education must enable man to become more efficient, to achieve with increasing facility the legitimate goals of life.' Here he points out two things: utility and culture. Utility indicates efficiency and culture implies legitimate goals of life. Having said this, our education system meets this requirement to a large extent. How do we make it better, is the question.

> He was so learned that he could name a horse in nine languages;
> so ignorant that he bought a cow to ride on.
>
> *– Benjamin Franklin*

There are no two ways about the fact that our education system is centred around excellence and scoring well in the exams. It is not built around what you want to do. Competitive examinations for the undergraduates and postgraduate courses, therefore, are highly structured and academic in nature. But let us call a spade a spade. If you have decided to be a computer engineer, then there is no way you can skip programing languages, operating systems, and subjects like computer fundamentals and Boolean algebra!

What I am trying to get to is that the fundamentals have to be taught and a student has to be assessed on these fundamentals, based on this teaching-learning process. You can make improvements to the learning process and also amend the examination system. But the system works in its present form. At the same time, it does not take care of the willingness to learn on the part of the students. How many students are there in the class for the love of it, or for that matter, for the love of learning? Most of them are there to acquire marketable skills which can get them a job. Obviously, you don't work hard, spend your parents' money, and your three years of youth, to remain unemployed thereafter! After all, education must fulfil the legitimate goal of life!

> A college degree does not lessen the length of your ears, it only conceals it.
>
> *– Elbert Hubbard*

All this is fine, but what our education system doesn't teach is passion – love what we do and do what we love to do. This missing link needs to be addressed so that students find their best fit in terms of their likes and their potential to achieve. I don't have any statistics to prove, but having been in the business of education, and having interviewed thousands of young boys and girls entering the portals of the best B-schools, I have come to realise that there are very few who study or educate themselves because they love to study the subject. In case of fine arts, film making, and creative fields, the number of people attending classes for the love of it may be much higher than those studying science, engineering, and business.

I feel that there is a need to connect at the emotional level. It is not only the educationists or the institutions that need to bring about a change, but a large part of it has to come from the students and their parents. Therefore, getting high energy levels into schools and colleges and the next generations is a joint venture, where stakeholders are parents, students, and the educational institutions.

> When I was a boy of 14, my father was so ignorant, I could hardly stand to have the old man around. But when I got to be 21, I was astonished at how much the old man had learnt in seven years.
>
> *– Mark Twain*

Role of Parents

Parents are the guides for their children and can do a number of things to make a change in their children's lives. Here is a what can be done.

- Find out what is your child's interest.
- Make it a habit to listen.
- Look at the telltale marks (listen to friends).
- Let them decide which stream to choose.
- Minimise criticism.
- Act like leaders.
- Set an example.
- Inculcate reading habits.
- Encourage adventure.
- Get involved in the education of your children.
- Don't make them overambitious.
- Teach courage.
- Encourage to experiment and be different.
- Contentment is the key.
- Handle mistakes.

- Don't protect too much.

- Boost general passion quotient.

Many of the parents are either not aware of some of these simple things that can infuse passion into their children, or are unable to implement these because of various reasons. These are not impossible to implement, in fact, these are very easy to act on, if you make conscious efforts. I will now elaborate these.

• What is your child's interest?

Sometimes this sounds too cliché. First of all it is not necessary that every child will display something very unique and extraordinary in his or her behaviour, which would put him or her in the league of a Mozart or a Picasso or an Albert Einstein for that matter, from the age of six! This is absolutely true and realistic for most of the children. Please understand that everybody who loves football at the age of 12 doesn't have to have a Pele in him! Children may love to play football because they just enjoy playing it.

If it is an extraordinary talent, then as parents, you don't have to look for it – It will be visible straight away from miles. Broader interests are what actually matter. For example, some children are studious and love to read a lot. Some of them show a great passion to achieve something, like getting into the government Civil Services, or being a pilot or becoming an aeronautical engineer. These broad directions are important pointers, and while guiding your children in the decision-making process, you must keep these in mind, and present a realistic picture to them. For example, if you see that your child is enthusiastic about engineering but you are sure he is weak in maths, then you must tell him that maths is the very basis of engineering and getting into it would be an uphill task. You should explain the linkage so that he doesn't make a serious mistake while choosing his career or subjects. This is career counselling at its simplest best.

• Make it a Habit to Listen

Today parents don't have the time to listen to their children. In fact, it should be a two-way communication.

If you don't communicate your feelings then how do you expect them to communicate back? Listening is often not an easy task. It is difficult to listen to bosses, peers, as well as subordinates – then what about poor children? They normally fall into the last priority. You should make it a habit to listen and allocate some time for it from your busy schedule. About three decades ago, the entire family used to have at least one meal together. During dinner time children used to share their concerns, their experiences during the day, or what happened at the school.

Today, each one of us is busy with so many other activities that we don't talk much to each other. This basic issue of breakdown of communication has to be addressed by the parents, if they want to guide their children properly, and infuse passion into them. Therefore, listen to the children and let them express themselves fearlessly. Listen to them without interruption and without judgement; when children express their feelings and experiences in words, they also improve their expression and their thinking process.

• Listen to their Friends

Friends are a great source of information. Friends are very close to each other and often share their likes and dislikes with each other. Talking and listening to your children's friends can get you some insights into your own child's way of thinking. Friends will be more open with you rather than with their parents, and they could also share with you the special insights that they may be aware of about your child. In fact, many a times these inputs will validate your own views about your children. For example, if you find your child to be studious and his school friends inform you that instead of playing basketball in the free period, he spends his time in the library, this would validate and confirm your own opinion about your child.

• Which Stream to Choose?

Every education system has its norms. In India, kids have to decide between science, commerce, and arts during their schooling. It is a decision of a lifetime. At this stage, it is more important to see the ability and flair of the child than passion. Remember, if you are good at something, passion is sure to follow. But if you take on something which you are unable to perform, then instead of enthusiasm, it would generate hatred and fear. Parents in their wisdom, many a times, advise their children to go in for something which can culminate into good career options later.

If parents have their way then every child would get into the science stream because that adds a great step towards engineering or medicine, which even today are the most sought after professions in India. Sought after yes, but are they the best choices? The answer is a big No. The service and knowledge industry provides the major boost to the national economy, and the options available are far more in number today than they were ever before. Hospitality industry, tourism, mass communication, technology, management, financial services, corporate training, operations managements, and event management, are a few of the thousands of options available today. Very few of them require science as a prerequisite. Today, the options are so many that one can easily experiment to find the best fit. All that the parents must do is to make them aware about their strengths and weaknesses, so that it helps the children make a realistic decision. Also don't force them into something they don't like.

Let me briefly explain what happened with my son. In school, he was an above-average student, and wanted to pursue science. I found him to be good in mathematics, so obviously encouraged him to go ahead. Neither he nor I were looking for a Thomas Edison in him. My argument being that knowledge of science at school level would improve his logical abilities and would not do any harm in particular. Having done well, again an above-averahe performance in school, he wanted to do computer science (I may have been his role model). He did his bachelors in computer science, did a decent job, but suddenly took a U turn. He found that it was not his cup of tea. That time software industry was doing well and he wanted to do anything else but a software job. Many of my colleagues advised me to advise him not to abandon computer science and try for MCS or MCA – the most lucrative qualifications in the domain.

My son's argument was simple, 'I don't hate computers but I also don't love it'. He had not found his love yet, but he knew what he probably hated. I couldn't agree more. He chose to go for human resource specialisation because he wanted to be into a management field. He didn't like marketing and hated finance. Again, a method of elimination, which made human resource specialisation a logical choice. I think when I look back, it was a sound decision because he is not only happy, he is loving it and doing well in his profession. I feel that as long as you follow the major goal posts and don't make the decision making too complex, you will be on target.

Never criticise a man until you have run a mile in his shoes. That way if he doesn't like what you have to say, it will be okay, because you would be a mile away, and you will have his shoes.

– Robin Evans

• Minimise Criticism

Criticism is the biggest passion killer. When you give a suggestion to your boss or raise a point in a meeting, and your boss starts criticising your idea and is not even prepared to listen; how does it feel? You feel miserable. Most of the ideas we are vocal about are very close to our heart. We are, to an extent, in love with these ideas which we feel should be implemented. If the criticism comes more than once, then most of us stop giving suggestions with an attitude, 'To hell with it'. Criticism gags people.

It has the same effect on children. They also cannot take too much of criticism. It is much more destructive in case of children than in case of adults. It has a long-lasting impact on a child's personality. Children are enthusiastic about certain things or activities at school as well as at home. Being enthusiastic is the first step towards passion. Repeated criticism would ensure that the child will loose his enthusiasm. It will dampen his initiative and inspiration for that activity. I remember we used to be very fond of making models in school. We used to use different materials, and spend hours in the workshop trying to make our own castles in the air. Our parents and teachers always encouraged us to build these models, which on the hindsight, seem ridiculous, in terms of standards and quality.

Sometimes when we didn't have money to buy the right material, we would improvise. Some of us were so crazy about building these things that we would totally lose track of time, and often worked late in the night to finish the task at hand. Imagine, with so much fire in the belly, if somebody criticised our end-product, how would we feel. Parents and teachers also criticise to make people conform to certain norms. While discipline, respect for rules and law are a must, making people too regimented also kills creativity. We criticise because we want our kids to behave in a certain manner. This way we will only produce conformists, who cannot be expected to have much enthusiasm.

And so it criticised each flower, this supercilious seed, until it woke one summer hour and found itself to be a weed.

– Mildred Howells

• Act like Leaders

Leadership is not only required in the political, military, or corporate scenario. Teachers and parents are our role models when we are very young. We look up to them for guidance, a nod, or an assurance. Remember that great leaders infuse passion into their people. Winston Churchill, John F Kennedy, Nelson Mandela, Lee Lacocca, and General Patton, are some of the leaders who stimulated their organisations and their countrymen.

Therefore, principals of schools, teachers, and parents, must demonstrate good leadership traits. These traits and qualities of leadership were best demonstrated by fathers and nuns of missionary schools, and children loved it. When parents demonstrate leadership traits, they not only earn respect of their children, but also become a guiding force for them. Good leaders inspire confidence and passion.

• Setting an Example

Enthusiasm is contagious. If parents demonstrate their inspiration and live their passion on a day-to-day basis, it is most likely going to rub off positively on the children. We as parents become a great source of inspiration for them. It has a far greater positive affect when they see you living your passion, rather than you telling them to do something just in words. If you are enthusiastic about doing yoga and pranayam in the morning and do it regularly at home, I am sure your children will watch you doing it and will try to emulate you some day or the other. I had a friend of mine whose father was a cavalry officer and was a very keen rider. He was a proficient rider and often played polo. Both his sons became fond of horse riding and learnt it at a very young age. On the dining table, horses, saddles, and riding were the favourite topics of discussion. They had a huge collection of photographs of horses, show jumping, and even used saddles for making their bar stools!

> Children have never been good at listening to their elders, but they have never failed to imitate them.
>
> *— James Baldwin*

Actually this is an action point for all parents. If you yourself do not have affinity for anything and obviously don't demonstrate it (because you have none, then how do you expect your children to be passionate about something. If this is so, then you got to find ways and means of getting your own passion out of the bottle, by reading this book once again. Look at the numerous suggestions given in the book which can make you identify your own passion. Let your own juices flow, and then let these transfer to your children.

> The best effect of any book is that it excites the reader to self-activity.
>
> *— Thomas Carlyle*

• Inculcate Reading Habits

With the advent of electronic media and onset of computers, reading habits have taken a backseat. The next generation has almost stopped reading general books. Unfortunately, today children read only books which are prescribed as textbooks in schools. Reading books on different subjects not only improves your expression, but also broadens your horizon. When I ask you to encourage reading, I am not suggesting that children should read very heavy books. Reading must be enjoyed, and one could pick up fast paced novels by popular authors like Sydney Sheldon, Arthur Hailey, Jeffrey Archer, or Frederick Forsyth. You always learn from these master storytellers. In fact, comics, short stories, and a variety of books are available for reading, and you must invest a little money every month to buy some books for your children and your home. It would not be a bad idea to build a small library at home. Don't insist on very serious books like classics to start with. The moment you tell your children that reading is good as a learning tool, there will be a resistance to pick up books. If you convince them that it is so much fun reading a book, then the ice will melt. The best way here is also to demonstrate reading habit. Walk your talk! If they find you reading a book with a lot of interest, then chances are that they would pick up the same book to read out of curiosity.

> I find TV very educative. The minute somebody turns it on, I go to the library and read a book.
>
> – *Groucho Marx*

Reading is like an addiction. Once you get hooked, you are hooked forever. Once this habit is formed, children will love to buy books and read on their own. The moment this habit is in place, encourage your kids to read biographies and autobiographies, which are great battery chargers. I remember how good I felt when I read Lee Iacocca's autobiography almost 20 years ago. Books on leadership, motivation, and human behaviour also must be encouraged. These should be our companions for holidays, excursions, and travel as a matter of habit.

Internet is a good tool to get information. Unfortunately there is too much stress on internet, which to me appears over-hyped. Students have stopped reading and have started copying by downloading information and submitting assignments by pasting these together. Nothing can replace reading from books and magazines and nothing can substitute one-on-one classroom teaching. So next time someone talks about WiFi and accessing the Internet while sitting under a tree – please think about it. Does it do any value addition?

It is only in adventure that some people succeed in knowing themselves.

– *Andre Gide*

• **Encourage Adventure**

In the earlier part of the book, I mentioned that we should develop a habit to try out new things. Read different books, try out different foods, and even different dresses. This breaks the monotony of everyday life. A step beyond this is adventure – which means venturing into unknown areas. Passionate people are adventurous and adventure builds excitement. How can you follow your passion and make it into a profession, unless and until you have that adventurous spirit! We must, therefore, encourage kids to go for treks, long walks in the woods, play different games, and get into adventure sports if possible.

Our activities should be such that children become adventurous, and acquire it as an attitude. Therefore, if your child wants to go out with his friends for a trekking expedition, don't stop him. Today, children are tucked into their homes during summer holidays, and are often playing video games in air-conditioned environments. They have been disconnected from rugged games like football, hockey, and basketball, leave aside mountaineering or hand gliding. We are making sissy's out of our next generation! How do you expect him to take a risk following his strong likes in life (which has some amount of risk involved), when he has never stepped out into the rain with a football, as it can get him a severe cold! It would be a good idea to attend summer camps which are now organised by professional organisations. The participants are taught rappling, mountaineering, and even river rafting.

I remember my son attending an adventure camp for a week where all this was done. He was just 14-years old when he attended it, and I was amazed at the transformation. One week of staying away from home in tents in the freezing cold temperature and following a tough timetable and managing things on his own, had a very positive effect on him.

If you are not living on the edge, you are taking too much space.

– Anonymous

• Get involved in the Education of your Children

Now this is a tall order in today's scenario. Most of the parents living in the urban areas are hard pressed for time. On an average, a person works about 10 hours a day. Add to it a travel time of an hour or two, and you have a 12 hour working day. While at home, you have number of distractions for the entire family — TV programmes, phone calls, Internet, DVD and so on. Today, we suffer from information overload, and we have no time for ourselves.

Nothing comes for free, and to kindle high energy into children also comes at a cost. If you want your children to follow their inspiration and be enthusiastic, then you got to get involved in their education. Remember, as I said earlier, parents are major stakeholders in the upbringing of their children. A child spends about eight hours in the school and the rest of the time is spent at home or with friends in the vicinity. Another important point is that a teacher has to pay attention to 40 children, whereas with parents, it is almost one-on-one. This leaves a much more deeper impact than school because of closer interaction.

Today, unfortunately, the parents feel that once they have paid the fees, their responsibility is over. They spend more energy monitoring the performance of the teacher, than that of their child! At the drop of a hat, they are there to blame the school and its environment, but are not even ready to put their penny's worth to solve any problem. In addition, they are overprotective! Is that all that is required to bring up children? I feel parents need to get involved in helping their children learn some subjects which are difficult. This can be easily done till class tenth because in the urban scenario, both husband and wife are literate enough to teach the main subjects. With this involvement, there is a sense of gratitude which the kids develop towards their parents. In fact, that has been the basic difference between the Western and the Eastern cultures. Most of the parents in the East devote more time to their children and their studies. Today, the trend is unfortunately reversing.

Apart from teaching academic subjects, parents need to teach life skills to their kids. These are those basics required to navigate in the world. For example, handling setbacks, negotiating skills, interpersonal communication, conflict resolution, and sharing and caring, are all best learnt at home, and that too with examples.

Let us not forget that over a period of time we have acquired a lot of skills and wisdom. Some of it is acquired by parents the harder way. You as parents must pass this on to the kids so that they are ready to face the world.

• Don't make them Overambitious

Whenever our ambitions grow they grow in the wrong direction, and we all become ambitious 'materialistically'. A big bank account, a swanky office, a well-paying job, a good car, and a big house. These are the stakes and we make our stakes very high. When you look at people in the corporate world working like mad, almost 14 hours a day, what do you think they are working for? They are working for these stakes! And the senior they become, the more insecured they are, because stakes are higher at senior levels. If you groom your children with a background philosophy that you have to reach the top because that is all that matters, then let me assure you, they may never find their passion in life. You have set their targets and you have set their means, then where is the room for passion?

If you have to follow your passion, then you got to be prepared for a bit of sacrifice in terms of your worldly ambitions. This point must be driven home while you bring up your children. Let them always be reminded that money is important but it is not everything, and this value cannot be taught at schools. This also needs to be demonstrated to the children by their parents. To quote John Abraham, the film actor, 'My parents are my role models, and have helped me keep my feet firmly on ground always'. On many occasions, he has said that his parents still prefer to travel by bus. They actually practice what they preach. Children of such parents would always be content and prepared to take risks in life and follow their hearts, because they are ready to travel even in a bus – if required. This is what is called as values – what we learn from our parents. It becomes a difficult proposition if parents are aggressively ambitious and set their sites too high. Their children will also follow suit. If you are one of those ambitious types, then try and review your philosophy so that your children are not the captives of these high stakes set up by you.

If you want to do everything right, then you will probably not do much of anything.

— Win Borden

• Encourage to be Different

Kiran Bedi was on our campus to address the students, and she was talking about individuality and taking up subjects like liberal arts. She explained the meaning of liberal art in a very simple manner. Liberal arts allow you to pursue something different than what you have been doing till now or all your life. An engineer can study music or painting. In a way, this stream allows you to pursue your passion. It also acts as a great value addition.

Dr S B Mujumdar, Founder, Director of Symbiosis, while addressing a gathering on liberal arts, said that, liberal arts may not give you a stand-alone qualification to get you a great job, but it will be a great value add. He explained the meaning of value add very beautifully, by giving the example of water. If you take a glass of water at room temperature and then heat it and bring it to the boiling point, then you have done a value add to the glass of water. Cold water and hot water look alike, but hot water has that value add in it. Passion is also a value add – it brings a different level of energy in you. You can't see the heat, but you can feel it.

If you want your children to be passionate, then teach them and encourage them to be different than others. They need not always follow the beaten path. Let them explore new avenues and opportunities. If they follow the footsteps of millions of people, then they will become one out of the millions – like anybody else. This doesn't mean being always distinctly different. You don't have to be distinctly different; you can be a doctor but be different from others in your approach. You can be a painter, but be a painter with a different style – a style of your own. You can be the CEO of a company, but develop your own style of leadership – a different style.

If you look at Kiran Bedi, she is the first woman Indian Police Service officer with a difference. She started Vipassana Meditation in Tihar Jail, which no one dared or even thought of. She always stood apart and put her heart into her job. Where do you think she learnt it from? In her own words, she learnt it from her father who always used to say that his daughters would be different from others. He encouraged them to be different, and his daughter grew up to be different from others.

• Teach Courage

Courage is not necessarily physical. Courage exists and manifests in many subtle forms. When you choose a career, you require courage, when you take up a job it requires courage, and when you quit a job because you don't like it, then also it requires great courage. There are millions of people working for a livelihood, many of them are hating what they do, but they do it day-in and day-out, because they don't have the courage to quit and follow their heart. Courage plays a very important role in following your heart. Parents play an important role in building courage in their children as a strand of character. Many a times children require your support and assurance, to choose a line of action. Ruppen Kapoor, the founder of Child Relief and You (CRY), who was a flight purser, wanted to quit his job to start CRY. His friends discouraged him, but his mother was very supportive in this mission. She in fact was the only one who asked him to quit his well-paying job and start CRY – follow his heart.

A ship is safe in the harbour, but that's not what ships are for.

– William Shedds

• Encourage to Experiment

How can you invent something new if you don't experiment? Experimenting should become your habit, and this becomes a second nature if taught from the childhood. Every experiment has the best and the worst outcomes. If an experiment is successful, it is the best outcome, but if it fails, then it is the worst. When you experiment, you should be mentally prepared for the worst outcome, and then be positive about it and go all out to give your best shot. Children brought up on such philosophy by their parents are sure to follow their hearts, because they are groomed this way.

Life is too short not to experiment.

– Jamelia

• Contentment is the Key

In today's environment of glamour and glitter, contentment becomes a very important virtue. It is important for us to learn how much we actually require to live well. On reaching a certain age, one realises that what one had been really chasing all through the life were false targets. Our goal setting in most of the cases goes haywire. We often set goals from our heads, and not from our hearts, because actually we are copying the goals of other people. Often we are not so worried about where we are going; we are more bothered about where others are going! This starts the rat race. As I said earlier, realise these things too late in the day when we have little time left to follow our heart and then we say/wish we had done the things we wanted to.

The lesson to be learnt here is to teach your children to be contented. Now this doesn't mean you are teaching them to resign to their fate and sit pretty, doing nothing. Contentment is a balanced state of mind. It is a fine balance between over achievement and achieving nothing – it is that mid path. People with such a mental makeup can afford to follow their hearts. They are really not bothered so much about achievement. They enjoy the journey more than the destination.

• Handling Mistakes

We all make mistakes throughout our lives. As long as we learn from our mistakes, its fine. The problem is when we don't learn from the mistakes. When we look at mistakes committed during childhood, then we can catagorise them in three specific forms:

- Careless mistakes

- Experimental mistakes

- Deliberate mistakes

Careless mistakes are those where there is some form of a casual attitude, because of which things go wrong. Here you got to tell a child that had he been a little careful, things wouldn't have gone wrong. You need not be very harsh, but the point must be driven home that one has to be careful – after all you are living in a real world where careless mistakes (which can be avoided if you are a little careful) should be avoided.

For example, if your child has forgotten his umbrella in the movie hall, you got to tell him to be careful the next time, so that he doesn't take things so casually the next time. Experimental mistakes are when the kids are trying out something new or there is a learning process. You cannot get annoyed with your child because he fell down while learning how to ride a bike or has made a mistake while noting a number on a note pad. But we do lose our tempers even when such mistakes are made. If these mistakes are frowned upon, then children will always be over-cautious, and sometimes even nervous to learn new things or experiment. Another way of looking at it is that, if the kids are prevented from making any mistakes during childhood, they would end up making bigger and costlier mistakes during their careers later. Deliberate mistakes are actually mistakes. They are designed to either create trouble, or achieve something wrongfully, and with a bad intention.

Deliberately losing the umbrella in the movie hall to annoy parents is not a good thing, and this behaviour needs to be corrected. Therefore, encourage experimental mistakes, but put a caution on careless, silly mistakes (which can be avoided) but reprimand for deliberate mistakes which are an attempt towards malice.

• Don't Overprotect or Over-provide

Lately the trend in parenting has been to protect and pamper the child. There could be two good reasons for this. First, people in the urban areas have started earning more than what they did three decades ago, and have enough disposable income to spend on their children. Second, since working parents have little time, they cover it up by meeting all the demands of their children. If you have the money, go ahead and spend it, but let your children realise the value of money. If this doesn't happen, then at a later stage in life, when you are not around, they will feel frustrated if there is shortage of money. We have also become very protective. This actually makes children mentally less resilient. Let the children fight their own small battles in life. Make it a habit for them to fend for themselves.

If your children can't manage their own affairs, require your support for everything – things that they need to do, then obviously they are not bold enough to follow their hearts. So don't make them so dependent that they are incapable of doing what they want to do. In other words, make them a little more mentally robust, and this will do a lot of good to them for the rest of their lives.

In earlier days, parents used to deny certain things to their children, like an expensive toy or an expensive watch. Children sometimes used to hate this. But this made them understand the value of money and inculcated delayed gratification. Today God doesn't make such parents because every parent wants to splurge on his or her kids. In the bargain, it negatively affects their character.

• Encourage Initiative

Many parents don't let children experiment or try out new things. This affects their attitude negatively. Count yourself lucky if your child takes initiative in doing things. For example, your child could well buy a sapling and surprise you by planting it in one corner of the garden. It may not have been the perfect spot to plant according to you, but the boy had taken an initiative of saving his pocket money, buying a plant, and digging a hole to plant it! If you don't encourage, at least don't discourage. If an initiative is curbed, then you can be rest assured that your child will not be enthusiastic about many other things that you want him to do.

• Fear of Failure

Who wants to fail? Therefore, we all fear failure to some extent or the other. If parents add to this fear, then obviously fear will become unmanageable and would end up with your child being overcautious in his approach for almost everything. This would kill his or her initiative. Therefore, always make a philosophy that, do your best and don't worry too much about the result. As Lord Krishna says in Bhagwad Gita, 'Do your Karma and don't expect anything in return'.

• Boost the General Passion Quotient

If children find their parents full of energy, ready to experiment, playful, and living their lives to the fullest, I can assure you that it has a very positive affect on them. If a child finds his/her parents always tired, complaining, and unenthusiastic, then obviously it sets gloom in him/her. What I am suggesting is that keep the atmospherics in mind, and keep pepping up the mood of your children all the time, and you will find that their enthusiasm levels will always be high. Good humour, outdoor activities, and outings, can keep the moral high. So make an all-out effort to keep the general passion quotient of the family high. Rest will automatically fall in place.

Most of the ideas discussed before are simple common sense. But all of them are not very easy to implement. I feel if you can make deliberate attempt to put some of these in practise, you would be shaping a good path for your children to follow their hearts, and be enthusiastic about what they do with their lives.

Role of Educational Institutes

> I am not a teacher, only a fellow traveller of whom you asked
> the way. I pointed ahead – ahead of myself, as well as you.
>
> – *George Bernard Shaw*

Passion is not restricted to schools alone. We all go through a meaningful education process from kindergarten (KG) to postgraduation (PG). If I have to ask what is the difference between training and education, there would be different answers from different people. I would simply say that training is related to a specific skill-set, whereas education is more of a holistic approach to develop the overall personality. That is why we sometimes say that so and so is behaving like an uneducated person. This means that education system should positively influence our minds and hearts. It must be able to make us curious, enthusiastic, and fire our imagination. Unfortunately, our education system is too learning-centric, and there is no effort made to generate enthusiasm and inspiration in the students.

There is no structured approach to generate passion in schools and colleges. But there is a need to encourage students to see the area of studies as good for their own sake, rather than just a way of securing marks and degrees. Unless we encourage and support individual passion, the students will not be able to identify their individual core competence and their own core. Students also need to be encouraged to develop as individuals, rather than a factory product. Schools and colleges also lack in grooming students in the area of like-skills, such as conflict resolution, self-awareness, negotiating skills, interpersonal relations, motivation, and values.

Here are some of the things that can be done by the people who are in the field of education, to whip up passion, and create individual personalities:

- Not reacting to the demand-supply syndrome
- Creating entrepreneurs
- Guest speakers to share their experience
- Group studies
- Helping each other in studies
- Event management by students
- Involve students in improvement activities
- Activity-based student committees
- Peer pressure of the right kind
- Book reviews and study of successful people
- Developing confidence through counselling

- Parent-teacher interaction
- Inculcating reading habits
- Love of learning

  Let us look at each of these areas in some detail:

  Colleges are places where pebbles are polished and diamonds are dimmed.

  – Abraham Lincoln

• Not reacting to the Demand-Supply Syndrome

I had said earlier that people study with a primary focus of getting a job. Not only this, they take up studies in those areas, where the job markets are hot today (sunrise industries), and predictably would remain hot for years to come. There are basically two things that go against this approach. First, that it is not possible for a trend to go on for a very long time, at least not for a lifetime--given that industrial trends come and go in a lifecycle spanning five to 10 years. Second, today so many options are available to make a choice from, that sticking to one field throughout your life may be restricting your own marketable potential. Therefore, education should be viewed as an enabler, which would help a person perform well in any job that he/she takes. The educationists must focus on this issue, while counselling the students for selecting their subjects. I am surprised to see electrical engineers, chemical engineers, civil engineers, and commerce graduates all making a beeline for software jobs, just because these are hot today.

• Creating Entrepreneurs

The emphasis should be on non-dependency on the government to generate jobs. Make yourself so capable that you can employ 10 more people in an organisation or business which you yourself create. Entrepreneurs require a fire in the belly, and the very idea of creating your own empire will light up the fire. The institutes should encourage the students to become entrepreneurs because it not only gives you control of the organisation but also allows to venture into an area which you like – 'follow your passion'. This seed must be shown at an early age, and thereafter nurtured all along the education process.

• Guest Speakers

This becomes a very powerful motivation tool. Guest speakers from different fields must be brought to schools and colleges to address the students. They can share their experiences, how they achieved what they achieved, and inform the students about the various options available. When students listen to successful people, they get motivated to emulate them. Here the idea should be to broaden the horizon of the students, and give them inputs on as many related fields as possible.

> Part of the American myth is that, people who are handed over
> the skin of a dead sheep (parchment) at graduating time, think
> it will keep their minds alive forever.
>
> *–John Mason Brown*

• Group Studies

When students study together to solve a given problem, it is a different learning environment. They not only learn to work as a team, but also learn their individual strengths. A project, for instance, requires in-depth technology study, market survey, getting funds for the project, and marketing the concept. In such a case, a student who has strong communication skills will develop the module for marketing the concept, and the one with financial acumen will go in for how to fund the project. This helps them achieve self-awareness and experience of their own strengths and weaknesses. Eventually, it pushes up the passion levels.

In case of good books, the point is not how many of them you can get through, but rather how many can get through to you.

— Mortimer Adler

• Helping Each Other in Studies

Students should be encouraged to help each other in their studies. Students who are good in mathematics, should help the weaker group. This will give a tremendous boost to the person who is good in a particular domain. This will, in a very strong way, indicate to him about his own passion. I have heard some successful people saying that they are successful in a particular field because right from childhood, they loved that subject, and they helped others with that very subject.

• Event Management

Students must be made to get involved in event management. Unfortunately in most of the schools and colleges, it is left entirely to the initiative of a student. I have also seen with experience that the same set of students keep participating in all the events, while many of the others just don't get involved. It is the job of the teaching fraternity to ensure that every student is involved in event management. It could be organising a water polo match, or a quiz competition, or a play, or even a picnic. This not only boosts confidence of an individual, but also lets him see what are his areas of interest and his own capabilities.

• Involve Students in Improvement Activities

Involving students to improve the school/college environment generates enthusiasm. It also adds on to the self-worth of the students. They feel their opinions are good enough to be implemented. A word of caution here is that these should be suggestive in nature, but the control and final decision should be with the teachers and the management. Too much of involvement can also create implementation issues.

• Activity-based Student Committees

In every school or college certain activities take place regularly. Some degree of responsibility has to be given to the students to make these activities happen. Therefore, students event/activity committees can be formed, and then a student can be made responsible for a particular activity. This can be exercised at the teenage, and the degree of responsibility can vary as per the level of maturity and age group.

• Peer Pressure of the Right Kind

Peer pressure has almost become a cliché, and I feel it has been over-hyped by the modern thinkers. We are blaming our peers for almost everything that is going wrong. We blame peers for drugs, rash driving, disrespect to parents, no regard for the law or discipline, pregnancy in schools and colleges, suicides, to even watching pornography!

Do you think that there was no peer pressure some 30 years ago? Yes it was, but the direction of peer pressure was right, and the pressure was taken in the right spirit. If my friend is good in football, let me beat him in the debate competition, or if he is better than me in physics, then I will beat him in English literature; that was the spirit. Today, the peer pressure is skewed towards brand names, acquiring most expensive stuff, and driving a car given to children by parents. Then we talk of self-esteem! First word in self-esteem is 'self', and it better be understood that way. It is your own personal achievement, and you own worth that is important, because that is all that belongs to you and you alone. Rest is all begged, borrowed, or stolen. I think this point must be clearly understood by parents and teachers alike.

Make good citizens who are individually proud of their own achievements, and not allowed to live on the laurels of parental money and their achievements. How do you generate passion on your father's money? How can you have self-esteem on the basis of your father getting a Magsaysay Award! Parents are going ga-ga over their kids and are themselves in a rat race – rat race to provide more than what is required in terms of more support and money. I have seen parents standing outside the air-conditioned classrooms in schools, with best quality cold drinks, pastries, and wafers for their kids, anxiously waiting for the class to get over so that they can hand-over the goodies a delay of a second! We are, in these cases, bringing up over-pampered children, and that is why there is no resilience, no tolerance, and no patience in them. Since everything comes easy, you can't take failures, you can't take denial, and you can't wait for your turn. Then you blame it on the peer pressure! This is an important part of personality building, and is more of character building. Without these basics in place, it is difficult for a person to be brave enough to venture out into the world and follow his/her heart.

• Book Reviews and Study of Successful People

I feel that there is nothing as inspiring as getting to know successful people. Fortunately, there is so much of documented history available about so many heroes, that we just need to tap into these resources to motivate ourselves. Biographies provide an instant connect with the high and the mighty. They take you into a different plane, and prove it to you that someone out there had been able to achieve all that. More importantly, these biographies also prove that you can also do it. They push your confidence as well as your passion.

Therefore, schools and colleges must initiate reading habits in students and allow them to read biographies of great and successful people as a part of the learning process. Biographies of entrepreneurs, corporate executives, social reformers, and political leaders, make a real good basket for reading. Students should be asked to do book reviews and presentations about these successful personalities. A student may do four book reviews in his three years at the college, but he would also listen to maybe 100 more students, and thereby learn about 100 more of such personalities. This is the power of proliferation, and the time spent on these activities, is time well spent.

• Developing Confidence through Counselling

Counselling by teachers should be twofold. It must try to find out the strengths and weaknesses of a student, and thereby by channelise his/her energies to the areas that he/she is good at, and the activities that he/she likes. Having done this, it is important to build up the confidence level of an individual, so that he/she has faith in himself/herself, faith to follow his/her heart; follow what he/she is good at. All of us need constant reassurance that we are on the right track, and students are no different. A word of praise and correct advise can really transform people.

• Parent-Teacher Interaction

As I said in the beginning, parents and teachers are into a joint venture of creating the next generation. Here parents are bigger stakeholders. So monitoring the class reports alone is not sufficient. There has to be greater interaction between parents and teachers. Many a times the parents-teacher meetings are a formal annual ritual where students put up a good entertainment show, but very little is taken up as action agenda.

Parents must involve themselves and be a part of the development process, along with schools and colleges. Cooperation is the key, wherein, parents and teachers together make a workable agenda, and ensure its implementation.

• Love of Learning

Today, a half-life period of knowledge is less than three years. Therefore, half of what you learn today becomes obsolete in less than three years! This is because of the simple fact that technology and concepts are changing at a rapid rate. You have system upgrades on computers, new value add services on mobile phones, new ways of getting information, to name a few simple ones.

On the job front also, changes are taking place very quickly, and got to be not only on your feet, but should also be willing to learn. Therefore, love for learning is very important for survival in today's world. This needs to be built into the children from school level onwards, and learning must become our second nature. I have suggested a few very important tips which need careful consideration and implementation often by parents and teachers together. For this to be successful, parents and teachers must have faith in each other, and work towards a common maximum programme.

• Inculcate Reading Habits

There is no substitute to the books, as far as learning is concerned. Schools and colleges should make special efforts to ensure that students read all types of books to broaden the horizon.

Let Us Recapitulate

- Barring a few flaws, our education system serves its purpose to a large extent. We have progressed very well as a society, based on this very education system.

- Our education system is centered around academic excellence and scoring good marks. It doesn't cater for creating enthusiasm and passion in the students. This needs to be deliberately looked into.

- Parents, teachers, and students, are the stakeholders in the education system. Therefore, we cannot leave the entire responsibility to the teachers alone. Parents must plan a more proactive role, along with the teachers, to bring a change. Students on their part must cultivate that love for learning.

- Parents can do a lot to generate enthusiasm in their children and some specific actions can be taken by them to bring about this change.

- Academic institutes and teachers can also follow some structured guidelines to make students more passionate about the learning process.

YOUR PERSONAL ROAD MAP

1. Do you think the present education scenario encourages passion in students? Comment about schools and colleges separately.

2. What can be done to generate passion at schools and colleges?

3. Do you, as a parent, make a conscious effort to identify and infuse passion into your children? If yes, how?

4. What five activities would you suggest to your children which can boost their enthusiasm in general, and passion about the things they love?

5. What are the three things you would like to change in the present education system, and why?

6. Take up the following activities as a parent:
    (a) Inculcate reading habits into your children.
    (b) Invest a decent amount of money every month to buy general reading books, and gradually build a library.
    (c) Visit your children's school once a month for the next six months, and interact with the teachers. Draw up an agenda from the points discussed in this chapter, and ensure its implementation between you and the school.
    (d) Interact with friends of your children to know more about your children's interests and strengths.
    (e) Make an effort to act like a leader at home.
    (f) Demonstrate to your children that you have some passion and you are living it.
    (g) Encourage your children to be different.

7. Suggest three activities that you would practice, that would make your children mentally tough.

8. Make conscious efforts to not overprotect your children. Gradually make them self-reliant and confident.

Education is more than a luxury; it is a responsibility that society owes to itself.

– Robin Cook

Passionate Leaders

Heart into the Matter

Task of a leader is to get his people from where they are, to where they have not been.

— Henry Kissinger

WHAT WE DID TILL NOW

All along till now, I have related passion to personal success and individual performance. I have presented some strategies and simple ideas to stimulate individuals, so that they can perform better, become more enthusiastic, and more efficient in whatever they wish to do. This needs to be done constantly, and from school onwards. Unfortunately, colleges and schools also don't pay much attention towards this aspect. Same thing happens at home where parents don't make conscious efforts to ignite passion into their children. Whatever happens, it happens more or less on its own.

In this chapter, we are looking at whipping up 'mass inspiration', and that is a major function of leadership. Achievers use their inspiration for their own success as individuals. For example, an actor who puts his heart into work gets a Filmfare Award or an Oscar. Similar is the case with a poet, a musician, a craftsman, a mathematician, a rocket scientist, a tennis player, a software programmer, or a human resource specialist, for that matter. These are all individual achievements.

Most of us don't work in isolation, and as individual islands of excellence. At some point or the other, we got to manage things, manage people, and take the lead to collectively achieve results. Which means we have to act as leaders. Good leaders or successful leaders are those who are so passionate about what they do, that they create some kind of a sympathetic resonance in others – they radiate energy which stimulates others. You can very well see this in good film directors. In fact, getting other people excited about something is what leadership is all about. Passion, therefore, is a key quality or a core value for effective leadership. Let me first explain what is the essence of leadership.

> Before you are a leader, success is all about growing yourself.
> When you become a leader, success is all about growing others.
>
> – *Jack Welch*

What is the Essence of Leadership?

People often get confused and mixed up between managers and leaders. Both of these have two distinct functions – one is to manage and the other one is to lead. Although totally different, these two, in most of the cases, need to be performed concurrently, to achieve results. What many people call leadership is really management. Strategy, planning, analysis, procedures and processes, targets, numbers, and quality are all managerial functions.

Leadership is emotional; it is to do with the heart and not the head. It is that soft but hot stuff. Enthusiasm is a word derived from Greek, which means 'having God within'. Passion and enthusiasm are the key drivers for leadership. If leadership is 'soft and hot', then managerial process is 'hard and cold' – hard facts, synthetic procedures, cold and calculative effectiveness. Great leadership is all about thinking with your heart, and it deals with dreams, feelings, excitement, purpose, pride, desire, care, and even love. It is not only corporate leadership that is to be seen in isolation, but across our lives in our families, communities, hobbies, schools, and life in general.

Unfortunately we in business schools produce more good managers than leaders. We teach business strategy, organisational development, quantitative techniques, business environment, intellectual property rights, branding, and advertising – but we don't teach passion and leadership. If at all we do it, we do it in the ratio of 80:20, 80 per cent managerial skills, and 20 per cent leadership traits. Leadership is about transforming people and understanding human behaviour, and that is at the heart of the matter.

Many of you would have heard of the fairy tale about the princess and the frog, where the beautiful princess falls in love with the frog. One day she picked up the frog and lovingly gave it a kiss, and poof! The frog changed into a handsome prince. In this story the kiss did the trick which enabled the frog to become all that he could be. It brought the best out of the frog. This is the definition and function of leadership, to get the best out of the people. Therefore, leadership is an art and not science. It can't be tutored, but it can be gradually imbibed and nurtured.

Leadership without Authority

Have you been a victim of a train accident, a flash flood, or a natural calamity? Even if you have been spared the agony of going through a disaster, you would have witnessed some of these on the television. You would, for instance, during a train accident, see a few people take charge. The accident site could be in a God forsaken place, with no official help available, and hundreds of dead and injured people to be taken care of. Yet a couple of people take charge and give directions to those who are not injured or mildly injured, to start moving things. These people demonstrate confidence and a sense of caring and motivate people to fight the situation. They inspire confidence. The best part is that, people follow them as if they were the leaders. It also demonstrates the 'look up to' factor, because here, desperate people look up to anyone who inspires confidence and can show a way out. Devastation by tsunami threw up hundreds of such leaders – actual leaders.

As mentioned before, leadership is a matter of heart and not the head, and in extreme situations, people need to look up to someone who can assure them of a solution. In our day-to-day work, the leader again has to inspire confidence into his people, that 'it can be done'! Yet another simple situation is when traffic lights do not function and there is no cop. What happens is a total chaos, and a huge traffic jam. Have you ever tried getting out of the car and take charge. Try it, it works. If you and your fellow passenger get out and give directions to people so that the traffic can get organised, people will listen to you. This happens because human nature is such that it respects those who are well-meaning and who can show a vision, and who care. The presence of a 'virtual cop' assures people that he will be able to solve the problem, and shows them a vision which in this case is getting out of this jam! A vision, and how to achieve the vision, is the leadership function; and let me tell you people are waiting for someone to take charge.

> The final test of a leader is that he leaves behind him in other men, the conviction, and the will to carry on.
>
> – *Walter Lippmann*

This is leadership without authority, and according to me, it is the highest form of leadership. Today, we have a distorted or a warped idea about leadership in business environment. Good CEOs are those who can generate more profits, meet the bottom lines, and deadlines. This is business excellence and not leadership. There is a difference between a leader and leadership. Leader is a position (authority), whereas leadership is an activity (moving people). It doesn't come with a title or a job description or a charter of duties, and it is not confined to the highest echelons of corporate hierarchy. Many a times, the truth is that a person in the role of a leader is well-equipped to run the company, but ill-equipped to lead the organisation.

Leaders don't lead alone; they create more leaders in the organisation to run the organisation. True leaders are the greatest servants. In the world of business, non-profit organisations, and even nation building, you will find great leaders who raise people who can go out and do what other people person could not do. Leaders actually maximise the capacity and capability of each and every person that comes in their sphere of influence.

Dr Mujumdar, the Founder Director of Symbiosis is probably the best example of a leader, who gets the best out of a person. I call his style of leadership as 'gentlemanly leadership'. He inspires by his actions, but lets people do things their own way as long as the work is done. This way, everybody tries to give his or her best to the organisation.

Leadership and Vision

The greatest job of a leader is to conceive a vision for the people and then, in the best possible manner, convince the people to reach there. Vision is also like a dream of what can be within the context of the greater purpose and values of an organisation. The most difficult part is to articulate it properly, with ample clarity and conviction. It has to be made visible, and has to have a definite shape – sharp and strong contours for it to be visible to any ordinary man. It is also important to show where the people are (the start point) and where they got to go (the vision). This makes it a teachable vision and a transferable vision.

A leader has to be onstage all the time. His body language, his eye contact, his every gesture, adds up to his conviction. Adolf Hitler rehearsed his speeches again and again, moved his hands in the air passionately, and delivered his speeches with deep Passion. He sold the idea of the Third Reich to the Germans, he showed them a destination – a vision. To fight Hitler and Fascism, Winston Churchill delivered equally passionate speeches, which mesmerised Europe and the rest of the world during the Second World War.

Leadership and Passion

The highest common factor between all the great leaders is passion. Look at Nelson Mandela, Abraham Lincoln, Walt Disney, or Mother Teresa – all of them without exception were highly charged up, and passionate about their vision. As John Maxwell said, 'Leadership is about influence – nothing more nothing less'. You can only influence if you are truthful, sincere, and full of integrity. Let me tell you that, without an honest commitment to the vision, you cannot be passionate. Good leaders are so committed and excited about their goals, that the whole lot of people stand by them. When a good leader resigns, their teams also resign, but when a boss resigns, the team rejoices!

> People ask the difference between a leader and a boss. A leader leads and a boss drives.
>
> – *Theodore Roosevelt*

You look at Adolf Hitler as a leader again. His vision and articulation of his vision was so compelling, that people called him *My Fuehrer* which meant My Leader. His commitment convinced people to the extent that, every individual became his personal follower. So much so, that this man who was so short and frail, could convince and mobilise tough army men and wrestlers to make his own personal army called 'Brown Shirts' or Storm Troupers, who were prepared to even die for him.

I would also like to mention that there is a difference between 'displayed passion' and 'actual affinity'. We often reward people on the face value, i.e., the way a person speaks, which is a serious mistake. True leaders combine their inspiration with absolute integrity, and that is what mobilises people to work towards the vision portrayed by them.

THE GREAT PASSIONATE LEADERS

We have looked at passion and its direct connection with leadership. Now let us look at leaders across the world, from different walks of life, who led nations, armies, industries, and people in general. Each one of them had a vision which was very close to their heart. From the lives of these people, we should be able to learn how they achieved what they achieved. More importantly, how they transferred their energy levels to thousands, and in certain cases influenced millions of people. This in fact is the most important act of leadership. You will very soon realise that these leaders mastered the art of motivating others, by communicating their vision to the people effectively, thereby making them equally passionate about the values they stood for. There is no one thumb rule for achieving this – they all employed different methods and skills to achieve the same result.

JRD Tata

> Probably no other family has ever contributed as much in the
> way of wise guidance, economic development, and advancing
> philanthropy, to any country as the Tatas have to India, both
> before and since Independence.
>
> *−100 Great Modern Lives*

A modest, well meaning, honest, and adventurous person, JRD Tata spent over 70 years of his working life in India. Born in Paris in 1904, he died in Geneva at the age of 89 in 1993.

After Tatas, so many big industry houses were established in India, but none could ever match up to it in terms of its ethical, and philanthropical approach to business. JRD Tata was the Chairman of Tata − the largest industrial group in India for 52 years, and nurtured it with all his dedication and zeal. He genuinely cared for the people and the country he belonged to. To establish and run an industry in a country which believed in controlled economy, was a big challenge, and JRD, as he was popularly known, raised his voice against the misguided policies which stunted the growth of industry as well as the economy.

Speaking at the age of 82 he said, 'My one sorrow and regret is that the government had from Jawaharlal Nehru onwards, not allowed many of us, imbued with enthusiasm and hope, to do enough'. He was awarded the Bharat Ratna, the highest civilian award, for his contribution to the country. In India, the term 'National Interest' meant all sorts of things to all kind of people. To JRD, it meant advancing the country's scientific and economic capacities.

> If your actions inspire others to dream more, learn more, do
> more, and become more, you are a leader.
>
> *− John Quincy Adams*

JRD started civil aviation in India in 1932. By 1948, he had made it an international airline. Money was never the driving force of his life. What propelled him was the joy of achievement. He undertook two flights to commemorate the thirtieth and fiftieth anniversary of his launching of civil aviation in India. Few people of his stature would have done something like this. His second flight was nothing short of extraordinary, which was from Karachi to Bombay in a single engine Leopard Moth at the age of 78!

After the flight, he said, 'This was flight to inspire a little hope and enthusiasm in the younger generation of our country. When they are 78, and I hope they all will live at least to 78, they will feel like I do, that despite all the difficulties, all the frustrations, there is a joy in having done something, as well as, you could, and better than others thought you could'. This reflected his passionate nature.

> Our chief want is someone who will inspire us to be what we know we could be.
>
> *– Ralph Waldo Emerson*

His joy lay not only in what he personally achieved but also in the achievement of the other individuals whom he had groomed, and who worked for him. He, in his 52 years of chairmanship of Tata Sons, had groomed people in his organisation, who had grown into corporate giants in their own right. Grooming leaders is a leadership function – remember.

Briefly, his guiding principles were:

- Nothing worthwhile is ever achieved without deep thought and hard work.

- One must think for oneself, and never accept at their face value, slogans and catch phrases, to which our people are easily susceptible.

- One must forever strive for excellence in any task, however small, and never be satisfied with the second best.

- No success in material terms is worthwhile, unless it serves the needs of the country and its people, and is achieved by fair and honest means.

- Good human relations not only bring great personal rewards, but are essential to the success of any enterprise.

He had this adventurous spirit of taking the lead and would always back an idea which was good for the masses and the country.

I start with the premise that the function of leadership is to produce more leaders, not more followers.

– Ralph Nader

In September 1939, when the war broke out a brilliant scientist from Cambridge, Dr Homi Bhabha, then on a holiday, was stranded in India. Tatas arranged for a Chair for him in the Indian Institute of Science, so that his talent could be fruitfully used.

Four years later, Dr Bhabha spoke to JRD about his wish to establish an institute for fundamental research in India. His argument was that if such an institute was established, India would not have to look abroad for its experts, but would find them ready at hand when the time came for nuclear energy to be applied for power production. This is how Tata Institute of Fundamental Research (TIFR) was established. Later when Dr Bhabha was made in-charge of atomic energy establishment in Trombay in 1957, he took 46 of his top TIFR scientists. India's Atomic Energy Programme could take of because off JRD's vision.

It was not just the funds that were made available by the Tata Trust to the TIFR in the early years that made this happen.

Equally important was the time and energy JRD personally gave to the institute in its formative years. JRD was a man, who right from the beginning, believed that good organisations need good people. He was especially impressed with the Indian Civil Service (ICS) model, where a brilliant graduate was trained in all facets of governance, and according to him, performed very well. On these lines, he started Tata Administrative Service (TAS), where young and brilliant people were selected on merit and later trained and groomed to perform multifarious tasks across the group. Tatas also established Indian Institute of Science Bangalore (IISc), Tata Institute of Fundamental Research (TIFR) and National Institute of Advance Studies (NIAS). These are the oasis of knowledge and research.

JRD was of the opinion that the chairman of a large group like Tatas should not waste his time in attending meetings. So, he decided to delegate it to able people. He remained the active chairman of Tata Steel and Tata Sons, and delegated powers to the professionals best suited for the job to run textiles, hydro, electric, and other companies. JRD was a die-hard patriotic and had his role model in Jamsetji who had given the House of Tatas its unique position in the country. He would not ask 'what enterprise is the most–profitable?', but 'what does the nation need?' If the answer was steel or a university of science, Jamsetji would fulfil the need.

Somebody once remarked, 'What is good for General Motors is good for America'. JRD thinks the other way round, 'What is good for India is good for Tatas'. JRD respected and emulated Jamsetji because Jamsetji was a man of great intelligence, a man of extraordinary vision. There are some very intelligent people, but they have no sense of the future – Jamsetji had that sense. Tatas all along were people-oriented philanthropists. But they also understood that philanthropy does not mean donating money alone. They believed that the trouble one takes over someone in need, often demands more of oneself than the giving of funds. The Greeks knew that and coined the word which is derived from Fil – Anthra – Pi, which means 'love of fellowmen'. JRD was always more than happy to help people.

JRD's contribution to education is phenomenal. He believed that without art and music, man is incomplete and he started the National Centre for Performing Arts (NCPA). He did this to give impetus to our great heritage in drama, music, and dance, which was gradually disappearing. The first task of the centre was to preserve and record the heritage, and the second task was to promote as far as possible, a renaissance of Indian dramatic arts, or performing arts as we call them. He was also the first one to recognise the responsibilities of business houses towards rural upliftment, and started the concept of 'adopting villages in the neighbourhood'.

Tata, under his leadership, has established hospitals, educational institutes of very high calibre, helped in building nations atomic energy infrastructure, rural development and family planning, besides giving a world-class industrial base, entering into production of almost all conceivable products for the Indian masses. When asked, 'What has been the most satisfying experience of your life?', JRD replied, 'The flying experience has dominated, and no other can equal the excitement of the first solo flight. Next is Air India, where I had the freedom to do what I wanted'. He was a keen sportsman and played golf, learnt skiing at 40 and kept skiing till the age of 84.

He was also very sensitive to human sufferings. Once when he saw a poor man crossing a road in Bombay, he said, 'Look at the poor man carrying probably all his belongings on his head'. He always wanted to help those who were less fortunate than himself, and this was reflected in all his actions for philanthropy.

All he longed for was to be remembered as an honest man who did his duty.

A leader must have the courage to act against an expert's advice.

– Anonymous

John F Kennedy

Efforts and courage are not enough without purpose and direction.

– John F Kennedy

John F Kennedy (JFK) has left an impact on the American politics and the life of Americans, as probably no other president of America ever could. After him, every president has tried to portray himself as JFK as he was popularly known. Richard Nixon, Lyndon Johnson, Jimmy Carter, and even Ronald Reagan, in many of their actions throughout their presidential tenure, emulated Kennedy in more than one ways. He influenced and inspired Bill Clinton to a large extent.

John F Kennedy was shot by an unknown assassin and died on 22 November 1963. Even four decades after his death, he remains extremely popular. ABC News poll rated him the second greatest president of all times. Even today, he scores more than 62 million hits on Google search, with a whopping lead over Brad Pitt and Tom Cruise, who are close to 38 million! During his times as the president, Gallup Poll got him the highest ever average approval rating of 70 per cent. He led the nation through a number of difficult situations, by motivating and influencing his team, as well as the countrymen, to give their best. Kennedy was hugely successful in transferring his vision and passion to the people of America. They say that crisis creates leaders, but there are many leaders who fail to stand up to the crisis. When John F Kennedy took the presidential oath in the sixties, the Cold War between the Russians and the Americans was at its peak. The United States had by then lost the advantage of being the only nuclear power – Russians having acquired the hydrogen bomb by 1953. Kennedy had a formidable and most unpredictable foe in Nikita Khrushchev as the head of Soviet Union, under whose leadership Russians had startled the world by sending up Sputnik, an artificial satellite. The unemployment rate in America at the time of his taking over was 7 per cent, and annual economic growth was less than 3 per cent, as compared to a huge economic growth of 10 per cent for the Soviets. The British empire and the French had lost their teeth and their empires were as good as gone with more than 20 nations winning their fight for independence. Fidel Castro, a total communist was in full power in Cuba. America at this time was groping to find the national purpose. These were difficult times for America, and Kennedy was at the helms of affairs.

> All this will not be finished in the first hundred days, nor will it be in the first thousand days nor in the life of this administration, nor even perhaps in our lifetime on this planet. But let us begin.
>
> – *John F Kennedy*

He, as a leader, chartered a course for his countrymen and the world in these difficult times – a course which the Americans would be proud of. Kennedy had a clear vision, which he could communicate to his people in a very lucid manner. He portrayed the big picture so well that, the nation stood behind him in the most united manner. This is the most important role of leadership. John F Kennedy was convinced that America at that point of time had to safeguard its boundaries from the Soviet Union. He was aware that how, just barely two decades ago, the British and the entire Europe was taken by surprise by the Germans. He didn't want history to repeat itself. If the United States was to avoid the dire circumstances in which Britain found herself in 1940, he knew that the American political leadership would have to step up its responsibilities. He wrote, 'Any person will awaken when the house is burning down. What we need is an armed guard that will wake up when the fire first starts, better yet, one that will not permit a fire to start at all'.

His vision promised 'Peace for the Americans and the World'. In fact, he became the guard of the nation. On 5 November 1960, John F Kennedy stated, 'For I know what happens to a nation that sleeps too long. I saw the British deceive themselves before World War II, as Winston Churchill tried in vain to awaken them, and while England slept, Hitler armed, and if we sleep too long in the sixties, Mr Khrushchev will "bury" us yet. That is why the next president. . . must be the commander-in-chief of the grand alliance for freedom'.

A leader's job is to show the people where they are, and where they ought to go. Kennedy did this job brilliantly. In case of a nation where your actions can have serious repercussions, it is good to consult others, and Kennedy did that frequently. He understood that it cannot be a one-man vision, when the canvas is so large. But once he had clarity, his vision was simple, direct, and memorable. Kennedy's inaugural speech was a historical landmark, and it began as, 'Let the word go forth from this time and place, to friend and foe alike, that the torch has been passed to a new generation of Americans, born in this century, tempered by war, disciplined by a hard and bitter peace, proud of our ancient heritage, and unwilling to witness or permit the slow undoing of those human rights to which this nation has always been committed, and to which we are committed today at home and around the world'.

His concluding remarks were equally resounding, and was a call to service on the part of his own countrymen and the people of the world: 'And so my fellow Americans, ask not what your country can do for you; ask what you can do for your country. My fellow citizens of the world, ask not what America will do for you, but what together we can do for the freedom of man'.

This speech touched deep down, the hearts of the people, and the last lines were the most memorable ones. This was the way Kennedy set out a vision for the Americans. People who are sincere and passionate are also the ones who break the rules. Leaders who leave a mark are those who question the existing norms, and often make radical changes. Winston Churchill, during the World War I, as the first lord of the admiralty, ordered that all ships of the British Navy should be powered by oil, and not coal – although Britain was rich in coal but poor in oil! They have the courage to shake things up and reform the organisation in the correct direction.

The time to repair the roof is when the sun is shining.

– John F Kennedy

Kennedy's mantras for success were to make big changes. The following points are worth noting:

- Be bold
- Stand your ground
- Be prepared to be flexible – you could review and revise your stand.

John F Kennedy also demonstrated a lot of resilience. He treated each challenge as an opportunity, remained resilient in the face of challenges, and was determined to find a way out when things went wrong.

His stint with navy as the lieutenant, in-charge of a patrol torpedo (PT) boat during the World War II was a great learning experience, which built his willpower and resilience. His boat PT – 109 was hit by a Japanese destroyer and he had to stay in water for days, which further aggravated his back problem. Finally, he and his men had to swim for miles to reach the nearby islands for survival. Despite these health problems, Kennedy worked long hours and was always approachable. Kennedy used to experience terrible bouts of backpain, during his tenure as the president of America, and was often on painkillers. He was hospitalised many times and used to go around the White House on crutches occasionally.

> A young man who doesn't have what it takes to perform military service is not likely to have what it takes to make a living.
>
> *– John F Kennedy*

The word 'charisma', is derived from the Greek word charisma or a 'gift'. People often feel that charisma is inborn. Either you have it or you don't. To a large extent, this is true. But John F Kennedy proved this presumption wrong. Kennedy was a charismatic leader. In fact, he transformed himself from a shy, awkward young man, to be one of the most charismatic personalities in the American history. Over a period of time, he developed, with efforts, the typical 'political sex appeal'. He showed his team that charisma can be developed.

For instance, he appeared very casual and relaxed in his TV interviews but used to rehearse his interviews, expected mock questions and things like those for hours, before the show. For good effective leadership, style and substance must go together. Only style won't work – substance is also essential. He may have learnt from Adolf Hitler who was a very quite, recluse, loner kind of a soldier in World War II, and later became the most charismatic person in the recent history. Hitler acted, reacted, rehearsed, and used his body language, and his modulation of voice to excite the audience. He used to put up his act with tremendous effort.

John F Kennedy had learnt that to influence people, you got to build an image. You may be sincere and passionate about what you are doing, but it is important that your audience gets the message and gets convinced. He mastered the art of communication. His conviction was that first of all you should believe in your own message or your vision. His main concern was his vision – that the world had to be made safe – and he totally believed in this. The second thing that one learns from him is that one should speak to the people and not over or around them. This means straight and from the heart. To demonstrate passion and sincerity, Kennedy would many a times give his personal example. This shows sincerity and brings authenticity into the argument. John F Kennedy also used to be very candid about himself. I feel people who are sincere, confident, and passionate about work, can afford to be candid. Cultivating candour is an essential part of leadership.

He learnt to manage the media, and in fact, used it to his advantage like nobody else. He would always project his enthusiasm, appear energetic (despite his back problems), with a lean but fit looking body. His enthusiasm was almost electrifying, if not infectious. He, in a nutshell, would be the best example of a passionate, committed chief executive, who transferred his passion and vision to his team and his countrymen.

> You never know what would hit you. A gunshot is the perfect way.
>
> *– John F Kennedy*

Unfortunately this proved to be true for him. John F Kennedy was shot dead.

Mother Teresa

> One of the greatest diseases is to be nobody to anybody.
>
> *– Mother Teresa*

Leadership is all about inspiring and motivating people to work towards a defined goal – a goal or vision the leader has conceived for himself. If John F Kennedy led the Americans and mobilised the people of the world to stand behind him for world peace by charisma and conviction, then Mother Teresa, with her dedication and her missionary zeal, mobilised people in large numbers, to work for those human beings who nobody was prepared to look after. She would be the finest example of demonstrative leadership – a style which was neither flamboyant nor very vocal. It was simply leadership by example, and leadership with passion and dedication, to serve the poorest of the poor.

If you can't feed a hundred people, then just feed one.

– Mother Teresa

Born in Macedonia in 1910, Mother Teresa left her parental home to join the Sisters of Loreto, an Irish community of nuns with missions in India. She taught at St. Mary's High School in Kolkata for more than 15 years, but the sufferings and poverty that she glimpsed outside the convent walls made such a deep impression on her, that she took permission to leave the convent and devoted herself to serve the poorest of the poor in the slums of Kolkata. Starting with no funds, she began with an open air school for the slum children. Voluntary helpers soon joined her and she also started getting some financial help from people. She started, 'The Missionaries of Charity', in 1950, whose primary task was to love and care, for those people who nobody bothered to look after. By 1990, there were over one million co-workers in more than 40 countries.

In her own words, her mission was 'to care for the hungry, the naked, the homeless, the crippled, the blind, the lepers, and all those people who feel unwanted, unloved, and uncared for, throughout society'. Starting with 12 members in Kolkata, today it has more than 4,000 nuns running orphanages, AIDS hospitals, and charity centres worldwide, caring for the refugees, disabled, blind, alcoholics, and homeless victims of floods, epidemics, and famine in Asia, Africa, Latin America, Poland, Australia, and North America. She made a home for the dying out of a temple, and her organisation was operating 517 missions in more than 100 countries by 1996. A day after the death of Mother Teresa, John Paul II said:

Missionary of Charity: This is what Mother Teresa was in name and fact, and there is no doubt that she was the greatest missionary of the twentieth Century. The Lord made this simple woman, who came from one of the Europe's poorest regions, a chosen instrument to proclaim the gospel to the entire world, not by preaching, but by daily acts of love towards the poorest of the poor. A missionary with the most universal language, the language of love that knows no bounds on exclusion, and has no preferences other than for the most forsaken.

In 1979, she was awarded the Nobel Peace Prize, 'for work undertaken in the struggle to overcome poverty and distress which also constitute a threat to peace'. She refused the conventional ceremonial banquet given to the nobel laureates, and asked that $6,000 funds be diverted to the poor in Kolkata; claiming that this money would permit her to feed hundreds of needy for a year! She stated that earthly rewards were important only if they helped her help the world's needy. She was awarded Bharat Ratna in March 1980.

She was against divorce, which she thought was an immoral act. She was also vehemently opposed to abortion, which she viewed as 'plain killing by the mother'. She believed in ecumenism and said, 'There is only one God, and he is God to all; we should help a Hindu become a better Hindu, a Muslim a better Muslim, and a Catholic a better Catholic. We believe our work should be an example to people'.

When she was asked, 'What can we do to promote world peace?' Her answer was simple, 'Go home and love your family'. In 1982, she could persuade Israelis and Palestinians, who were in the midst of a war to ceasefire long enough, to rescue 37 mentally handicapped patients from the besieged hospital in Beirut. She travelled to help the hungry in Ethiopia radiation victims of Chernobyl, and earthquake victims of Armenia. After almost 40 years of work in India, she went to her native place in 1991 to open a Missionaries of Charity Brothers Home in Tirana, Albania. Mother Teresa was consistently found by Gallup to be the single-most widely-admired person, and in 1999 was ranked as the most admired person of the twentieth century. She once said, 'Loneliness and the feeling of being unwanted is the most terrible poverty'.

She died in 1997 at the age of 87, most of which were spent helping those who needed her the most. She was given a state funeral by the Government of India, an honour normally given to the presidents and prime ministers, in gratitude for her services to the poor of all religions in India. Her funeral ceremony was simple, but magnificent, and attended by queens, first ladies, and heads of state. Even the poorest and the disabled came to pay their homage to Mother Teresa, who had spent all her life in their services. The most touching moment of the funeral service was when a disabled and deaf man approached the casket; walking with very great difficulty, and touched the casket with trembling hands. This was the message of Mother Teresa, 'Direct, immediate action, caring, love, and the hell with the ceremony, tradition, pomp, and show'. The former UN secretary General Javier Perez de Cuellar, at her death said, 'She is the United Nations'. The world acknowledged that she was a rare and wise individual, who lived long for higher purposes.

Some people tried to compare the service with that of Princess Diana's, who had died a week earlier. Diana's world was mostly of glamour, and Mother Teresa's world was mostly very close to the humble ground. Diana danced and Mother Teresa merely cherished life, the life of others. In the end, Diana was a lost soul who struggled to find meaning in life and Mother Teresa gave meaning to life. Mother Teresa was a silent leader who inspired people to walk along with her by her direct action, care, and love.

Do not wait for leaders, do it alone, person to person.

– Mother Teresa

General George Smith Patton

May god have mercy upon my enemies, because I wont.

– George S Patton

Flamboyant, brash, and courageous, General Patton was the most colourful of the US Army's Commanders, during the World War II. He was a genius in tank warfare, and behind his showmanship and audacity, lay the shrewd judgement and imaginative planning, which made him the most formidable of generals during the Wr. He had passion, he had guts, and he loved glory, which was backed by solid professional acumen. So much so that when Patton's formidable Third Army was not committed to operation Overlord (invasion of Normandy to liberate France) and kept in reserve; the German high command, and even Hitler thought that Normandy (where the allied actually struck) could not be the primary invasion site if Patton was not committed to the battle! A major decisive strike was unimaginable without Patton, even for the enemy.

Hitler, therefore, kept his panzer divisions held back in reserve, only to be released where Patton would strike! German macro-level strategy was thus, 'Patton centric' in the most crucial battle of Europe. Patton was a diehard soldier at heart and had a leadership style of 'catching the bull by the horns' and always leading from the front. A soldier, general, pilot, athlete, gun owner, a hero, and a legend – George Patton, right from his childhood, wanted to become a war hero. He wanted to be where the action was, and wanted to be a fighting general. He had learnt to read military topographic maps by the age of seven, but didn't bother to learn to read till 12 years of age. A keen sportsman, he represented his country in the 1912 Olympics at Stockholm in modern Pentathlon.

As a general also, he was always there with his soldiers right at the front. Fighting was in his blood, and he had a passion to win. He would display his valour even when he was not in the battlefield, and in one such incident, while going for a formal dinner, he leaped out of his car and drew out his pistol to save a woman from three men who were abducting her.

His first major taste of war was during his command of the 1st US Armored Corps, which was to go for action in deserts of North Africa. A strict disciplinarian and a hard task master, he drove his troops very hard, sometimes expecting them to go without sleep for more than two days at a stretch. General Eisenhower, the supreme commander of the allied command, had great faith in him. Americans had suffered a disastrous defeat and Eisenhower wanted a commander who could turn around the situation, and he chose Patton to head the 2nd Corps which had suffered the defeat. His first job was to restore the moral of his dispirited troops, and pull up the officers who he wanted should lead from the front.

> I am afraid of an army of hundred sheep led by a lion than an army of hundred lions led by a sheep.

> – *Talleyrand*

According to him, 'A man of diffident manner will never inspire confidence'. His hard-nosed discipline, leading from the front, and being where action was, succeeded in getting his troops combat ready in a very short time. Patton was famous for his ivory-handled revolvers, which became his trademark. His actions and attire assured his troops that they were commanded by a fighting general. This earned him loyalty and respect of his men at all levels. He once said, 'I am a soldier. I fight where I am told to and I win where I fight'. He was later given the command of the 7th Army in 1943 to lead an invasion of Sicily. Even as a commander of an army, he put his command principles into practise by going ashore and personally taking charge on the beach in the middle of the battle. Mere presence of the commander can give a tremendous boost to the morale of a fighting army, and Patton never ever missed a chance. Germans feared him above all other allied generals. When he was sent to Corsica, the Germans were convinced he would lead an invasion of France. When he was sent to Cairo, they feared an invasion through the Balkans. Such moves of Patton caused the Germans to tie down a large number of troops to counter the Patton bogeyman. One man's presence could scare the hell out of the enemy.

Wars may be fought with weapons, but they are won by men.

– George S Patton

A man of action, he moved his 3rd Army very swiftly against Germans at the end of the war, covering 600 miles in two weeks. During the most difficult times of the battle, he could come up with radical ways of launching attacks on the enemy, and his troops always stood by him to give their best and perform even the impossible for their leader. He once said, 'If everyone is thinking alike, then someone isn't thinking'.

His 3rd Army finally consisted of more than half million men who had liberated or conquered 81,522 square miles of territory, and inflicted more than 14,00,000 casualties on the enemy (In fact he was outspoken and often spoke out of turn.) Patton was not a diplomat; he was a simple soldier who loved his profession, had mastered it, and inspired his troops by convincing them that they would win.

Patton died not of any gun wounds in the battlefield, but in a car accident in December 1945. He is still considered the greatest military commander in the US history. Even today, the 3rd Army veterans proudly announce that they served under Patton. He succeeded very well in being a leader of his men, a warrior, and a hero.

In military leadership, the vision is victory, and the leaders don't have much choice. They have to fight the battle wherever they are told to. But good military leaders are those who inspire confidence by setting personal examples and involvement, and demonstrate their resolve to the men, because every military venture is an adventure.

Success is how high you bounce when you hit the bottom.

– George S Patton

Sir Richard Branson

I never went into business solely to make money. I always said that I wanted to be the best rather than the biggest. At the end of the day, it all comes down to people; nothing else even comes close.

– Richard Branson

There would be very few people in the world who could match up with the enthusiasm and passion of Richard Branson – Passion to experiment and live life to the fullest. Called an 'insanely sane maverick leader', Richard has a US$5 billion business empire, with 200 companies across the world, delving into a large number of business domains. This man who is always ready for ventures and adventures holds records for being the fastest to cross the Atlantic Ocean by boat, the fastest to cross the Pacific, and the first to cross the Atlantic in a hot air balloon.

He clearly demonstrates that, to follow your heart, you got to have a streak of adventure in you. He truly has plenty of guts and a diehard spirit of adventure. An entrepreneur who started rather early, Branson launched a national magazine titled Student at the age of 16. Within three years, at the age of 20 he founded a brand name Virgin – A brand name which he is highly possesive about, with the launch of a record retailer, and a short while later, opened a record shop in Oxford Street, London. Richard Branson's ambition is to make it as popular as Coca Cola! Growing vertically he went into establishing his own recording studio in England, where the first Virgin Artist, Mike Oldfield, recorded 'Tubular Bells' which was released in 1973. His first album under the banner of Virgin Records sold more than five million copies. In the years to come, he signed up many superstars like Belinda Cartisle and the Rolling Stones.

By 1992, the Virgin Music Group and its recording studio was sold out to Thorn EMI in a US$ 1 billion deal. The Virgin Music Group, under his leadership, expanded into international mega store for music retailing, book publishing, film editing, and clubs and hotels. Virgin Atlantic Airways was started in 1984, and is now the second largest British long-haul international airline. His mantras for, 'Hire the best. Create energy around a goal. Lead from behind and expect people to achieve goals. Be a catalyst to the success of others'.

Richard always mixes adventure with business ventures. He rekindled the spirit of Blue Riband, by crossing the Atlantic

Ocean onboard his boat, 'Virgin Atlantic Challenger', in the fastest recorded time. A year later, he crossed over the Atlantic Ocean in a hot air balloon called the 'Virgin Atlantic Flyer' – reaching speeds in excess of 130 miles per hour. Yet again, in 1991, he crossed the Pacific Ocean from Japan to Arctic Canada, a distance of 6,700 miles, breaking all existing records with speeds up to 245 miles per hour in a hot balloon, measuring 2.6 million cubic feet. Having so many records of speed and adventure under his belt, Richard Branson also has an insatiable appetite and a desire to start new businesses. He loves challenges, especially when he enters a market that is dominated by a few major players.

Over three decades, he has created one of the most recognisable brands in the world. He focuses much of his attention on Britain, and he has been able to 'Virginise' – as he calls it – a very wide range of products and services. His brands of course have travelled across the world, with a strong presence in the US, Australia, Canada, Europe, and South Africa.

> Only go into new markets if you passionately believe you can turn it on its head.
>
> *– Sir Richard Branson*

Richard Branson, when asked during an interview, 'Did you ever let your heart rule the head?' replied, 'Ah the time–I think that unless you do, you're not going to be a very good business person. The only really good reason for doing things in business are based on what your heart tells you, not your head'. His another mantra for success which smells of high adventure is, 'Follow your instincts, and look before you leap'.

In 1999, Branson received Knighthood and became Sir Richard Branson for contribution to entrepreneurship. Does the Passion stop at hot air balloons? The answer is a big NO.

Branson has set up Virgin Galactic, which will make space tourism a reality, and at an affordable price.

Richard is short statured, but you don't notice it because he never stands in one place long enough for the necessary comparison! 'I keep my notebook in my pocket all the time, he says,' and I really do listen to what people say—even if I were out in a club at 3 a.m., and someone's passing on an idea in a drunken slur. Good ideas come from everywhere, not only in the boardroom'.

His advice, 'If you can run one business well, you can run any business'. Virgin Galactic has space adventure plans to fly passengers to an altitude of over 100 Kms, a space voyage where they would experience an total weightless time of a few minutes. Though the plans to build the space craft were conceived in 2005 the mission is yet not complete for a safe launch as of September 2104.

This once launched, will be an out of the world experience where passengers will be able to see the sky changing from cobalt blue to mauve then indigo and finally pitch black. Passengers will be put through 4G experiences, with an initial thrust of 600 mph being achieved in less than 10 seconds! They would see stars in the day time literally.

The mission so passionately conceived has been constantly facing technical challenges and the plans to have the first group of passengers fly in 2011 has now slipped to 2015.

This lifetime experience will cost $250,000. Only a maverick like Richard Branson could even think of something like this.

Can all this be thought out without an adventurous heart? No way. Thus, this is what Sir Richard Branson is all about – Passion, adventure, and vision, who will give you a pie of the sky. Thinking out-of-the-box, and thinking out-of-the-world, Sir quite a journey from marketing of records to space tourism!

Leadership is All About Influencing People

Looking at the styles, commitment, and achievement of these five great human being, one would conclude that all of them had a passionate commitment to a cause. They were also able to mobilise people behind them, by beautifully articulating their vision to them. They demonstrated commitment by their deeds, and had absolutely unquestionable integrity towards the cause they stood for. These people left impact on the lives of a large number of people, and influenced the masses with their achievement. They all had different styles and different means – but they were all spurred by a vision, and were committed to it. This is my definition of leadership.

Let us Recapitulate

- What we did till now

  We till now have related passion to personal success. It is important to look at passion which can whip up 'mass inspiration'.

- What is the essence of leadership?

  Leadership is emotional. It is to do with the heart and not the head. It deals with dreams, excitement, pride, and desire.

- Leadership without authority

  When people take charge of situations without having authority. This is the highest form of leadership.

- Leadership and vision

Good leaders articulate their dreams well and are able to convince others about the common goal.

- Leadership and Passion

The highest common factor between all the great leaders is passion.

  ◊ The great passionate leaders are:
    – JRDTata
    – John F Kennedy
    – Mother Teresa
    – General George Smith Patton
    – Sir Richard Branson
  ◊ Leadership is all about influencing people. Great leaders can visualise their dreams so well that they are able to mobilise people behind them.

'Leadership is the capacity and will to rally men and women to a common purpose and the character which inspires confience.'

– Bernard Montgomery

YOUR PERSONAL ROAD MAP

1. Pick up at least three most important qualities of each of the five leaders discussed in this chapter and make a consolidated list. Then pick up three most important of these traits, and try to use them in your life.

2. List five great people who were successful because of a great vision.

3. List five great people who were successful because of their passion.

4. Grade yourself on a scale often as far as passion and enthusiasm are concerned.

5. Do you have a vision of your own? If yes, what is it?

PQ Test

'A person with High IQ and a low PQ is more likely to underperform. Whereas, a person with low IQ but a high PQ is likely to excel in life.'

It is difficult to measure PQ and is still more difficult to assign it a number. The second difficulty that arises while looking at PQ as an intelligence is that, it cannot be viewed as an open-ended or a generic entity. As Howard Gardner in his decisively original work, *Frames of mind* mentions that all human beings possess not just single intelligence, many times referred to by psychologists as 'g' or general intelligence. Therefore, as humans, we can be better described as species having a set of relatively autonomous intelligences. PQ must be, therefore, measured or ascertained with respect to a particular activity or action. This activity or action should be identified as one's passion. The test must be applied on that particular domain. Here we are looking at a specific attribute or affinity to a particular domain, and not general enthusiasm.

For instance, if I feel, perceive, or presume, that my passion is music, then I must apply this test for music. The result thereof should give me an idea about how passionate I am about music.

With this in mind, you need to take this test. You should first identify your interest, and then answer the questions with respect to that interest.

These questions have been framed to assess your ability with respect to your passion on majorly five parameters as under.

(a) Your ability to learn and excel in that area.

(b) Your ability to earn a decent living from your chosen passion.

(c) Your attitude towards your passion.

(d) Your level of creativity in the realm of your passion.

(e) Your ability to put in sustained hard work to make a success out of your passion.

My passion is, for example, _____ _____ (writing/music/driving cars/painting/business/earning money/learning)

Rate each of the question or statement on a scale of one to 10, with respect to your passion stated above:

1. How energetic do you feel when you think about this? _____

2. How energetic do you feel while you actually perform this activity? _____

3. Does this activity attract you? _____

4. Are you prepared to walk an extra mile (make additional efforts) to perform this activity? _____

5. How much are you prepared to stretch yourself out of your comfort zone, to perform this activity, or achieve this? _____

6. Would you like to do this even if you have a comfortable income coming from other means? _____

7. You are in love with this activity? _____

8. You are in a state of ecstacy or nirvana when you perform this activity? _____

9. You do not get tired of doing this again and again? _____

10. It is easy for you to learn this activity from someone or a coach? _____

11. It gives you happiness. _____

12. It gives you satisfaction. _____

13. Do you feel you are having fun while you are in it? _____

14. Are you prepared to take risk in order to pursue this passion? _____

15. How good are you at this activity? (your perception) _____

16. How good are you at this activity? (other people's perception, you friends, family, and other's) _____

17. Do you think if you pursue your passion, it will help a few people or society in general in some way? In other words, will the outcome be of use to some people. _____

18. Have you made efforts to learn or work on your passion by reading, or by taking some coaching, attending seminars or similar performances by others in the same field? _____

19. How much are you focused on your passion? _____

20. Do you feel you are competing with yourself while you are living your passion or doing stuff related to your passion? In other words, do you like to make constant improvement in this specific field? _____

21. Are you prepared to tone down or make some sacrifice in your lifestyle, and worldly comforts, in order to follow your passion? _____

22. Are you flexible or can you remould yourself with respect to your passion? If you love painting roses, are you prepared to paint horses if people want? _____

23. Do you believe in yourself that you are good at this activity or interest? _____

24. Are you prepared to take a setback, financial or otherwise, which you may get while you are pursuing your interest? _____

25. How much adaptable are you towards your passion? This means you are prepared to work under different, and even difficult circumstances, when it comes to your passion. _____

26. You do not care that your academic qualifications would go waste, if you follow your passion. _____

27. Do you take pride in your passion? _____

28. Do you want to be the best, or do very well in your perceived passion? _____

29. Do you think you will be able to sustain this passion in the long run? _____

30. Do you have plans of achieving some of your goals in life through your passion? This goals could be happiness, contentment, or peace of mind. _____

31. Do you think you have this in you as a gift of God? _____

32. You do not bother about what others think about you pursuing your passion. _____

33. Do you think you can make a decent living out of this activity? _____

34. Are you willing to learn (this activity) from others? _____

35. You think you will make it to the top one day? _____

36. Do you read books, articles, and magazines related to your interest? _____

37. Do you make plans or make efforts to develop your passion into a marketable skill? _____

38. Do you have your own style of doing things in relation to your passion/interest? _____

39. How frustrated do you feel when you are unable to fulfil the desire of implementing your passion or your liking? _____

40. You like to experiment with your passion. In other words, you try different things within this domain. _____

41. Do you have a child-like persistence regarding your passion? _____

42. Do you get totally engrossed and involved with any activity related to your passion? _____

43. Do you demonstrate or have spontaneity while pursuing your passion? _____

44. How creative are you within the realm of your passion? _____

45. Do you have a natural tendency to make friends with those who have similar interests? _____

46. Are you rebellious as regards to your passion. You want to oppose people who are opposed to your following your passion. _____

47. You have a role model in the field of your passion – some one who is very good at it. How much are you in awe of him/her? In other words, how much do you look up to such a person? _____

48. You are prepared to bash on regardlessly, and pursue your passion, even if people criticise you regarding your passion. _____

49. You feel you have a deep love for your passion and it is not an infatuation. _____

50. You are prepared to learn from your mistakes with respect to your perceived passion. _____

Total: _____

Interpretation of results.

Please total up your score for all the 50 questions.

a) Score between 350 – 500.

You are very much inclined towards this activity or desire. If you pursue this, you have very strong chances of success. If this activity can be transformed to a commercial activity or profession, you can expect spectacular results. It is highly recommended that you pursue this desire without hesitation. Start making serious efforts, and invest your time in this activity.

b) Score between 250 – 349

Yes, you do like this activity. First of all you must try out this activity for some time, to perceive as to how much you actually like it.

This is known as the 'test drive' phase. This will give you an idea as to how much should you bank on this desire, and should you finally keep persuing it in future also.

c) Anything below 250.

You need to reconsider whether this activity is something which you really desire, or you are only in love with its name. This does not seem to be your cup of tea; but nevertheless, you can try your hand at it for some time. If you can stick to it for a reasonable time period without getting bored or sick of it, you may be lucky. Only in that case, you should spend time and effort to pursue this activity. If you get bored or tired of it, you can take a call and look for something else that may interest you.